PHOTOCOPIABLES

for early years

OURSELVES

EDITOR

Susan Howard

ASSISTANT EDITOR

Lesley Sudlow

ILLUSTRATOR

Lorna Kent

COVER

Lynne Joesbury

SERIES DESIGNER

Sarah Rock

DESIGNER

Sarah Rock

AUTHOR

Sally Gray

Published by Scholastic Ltd,
Villiers House, Clarendon Avenue,
Leamington Spa, Warwickshire CV32 5PR

© 1999 Scholastic Ltd Text © 1999 Sally Gray
7 8 9   3 4 5 6 7 8

British Library Cataloguing-in-Publication Data
A catalogue record for this book is available from the British Library.

ISBN 0439-01708-4

CONTENTS

TOYS

CLOTHES

FOOD

INTRODUCTION

Using themes

The *Themes for Early Years Photocopiables* series builds on and supplements the existing *Themes for Early Years* series, providing a rich source of material for topic planning and delivery.

Ourselves is designed to link closely to five of the original *Themes* titles – *Myself; Homes; Toys; Clothes* and *Food* – building on the ideas and providing additional material to broaden the scope of each topic. While the books may be used together, *Ourselves* is also a useful resource in its own right.

The theme of *Ourselves* is an established favourite for early years children. At this young age, children are self-centred and often eager to talk about themselves and their experiences. This provides valuable information for adults who can quickly learn about the children in their care. It is also an excellent way for the children to develop confidence in their pre-school environment.

How to use this book

This book combines the original *Themes* titles *Myself; Homes; Toys; Clothes* and *Food* in one book. Each of these sub-themes has its own chapter, providing fifteen photocopiable activity sheets and three pages of accompanying teachers' notes. The activity ideas are simple, effective and child-friendly, giving clear, concise instructions and allowing the children enough space to explore their ideas.

The activities in this book are clearly linked with QCA's Early Learning Goals. They comprehensively cover the six areas of learning and every learning objective closely matches the QCA document, enabling you to monitor your coverage of the curriculum. In addition, the activities provide clear and valuable opportunities to assess the children. The teachers' notes offer a complete lesson plan for each photocopiable sheet, explaining how to use the sheet and how to introduce, conclude and differentiate the activity.

Using the photocopiable sheets

To maximize the potential of the activity sheets, it is important to use them in conjunction with the accompanying teachers' notes. The notes will not only explain the main use for each sheet, but will also provide suggestions for introducing, differentiating and reinforcing the concept. The children will benefit more from the work if the sheet is presented with some adult input and often they are intended for groups or pairs as well as individuals.

The photocopiable sheets are designed to be used in a number of ways. There may be suggestions to enlarge the sheet, and copy it onto card or coloured paper. You may also choose to laminate some of the sheets, particularly those that will be used as games or for visual stimuli to promote discussion.

Many of the photocopiable sheets may be used several times, as they have been written as open-ended tasks and can be reapplied with a new theme or subject matter. For example, some of the sheets are designed to be used in role-play settings and provide templates for the children to use on a regular basis.

Several of the mathematics activities can be used with a different number or mathematical operation focus or as games.

Assessment

Date and keep copies of some of the photocopiable sheets once the children have used them. They are an important assessment tool and can be kept as records that demonstrate your coverage of the curriculum. You may also like to plan an assessment activity in advance, using one of the sheets as a way of recording the children's progress. For example, if you are planning to assess the children's ability to use letters and symbols to convey meaning, use the 'Teddy surprise' activity (see page 49) to note how confident they are in their ability to represent their ideas in letters and pictures. Date the work and add your own notes on the reverse.

Resources

The activities in this book have been designed to be used with a broad range of materials and resources readily found in early years settings, including collage materials, pens and pencils, scissors, malleable and construction materials and simple tools, such as scissors and tapestry needles. The photocopiable sheets will provide the children with many opportunities to develop a broad range of essential early learning skills from making books, to puppets and games and even a wiggly caterpillar (see page 95).

Links with home

The theme of *Ourselves* has many natural links with the children's homes and families. Through these activities, the children will have opportunities to learn and talk about their home, their friends, their family and household routines. The photocopiable sheets make it easy to share this work and include the children's own families in their learning and discovery. Let the children take some of their finished work home with them and occasionally send home some of the activities for the children to share with their parents or siblings. Make sure that you have talked to the parents about the learning potential of the activities, but explain that the activities, although educational, should always be made fun, with an emphasis on play.

MYSELF

PAGE 10
KEEPING CLEAN

Learning objective
To talk about personal hygiene. (Personal, Social and Emotional Development)
Group size
Whole group.

Enlarge the photocopiable sheet to A3 size and display it on an easel. Make sure that everyone can see the pictures. Mime an action from one of the pictures and ask the children to guess what you are doing. Ask one child to point to the correct picture. Now invite individual children to mime a picture for the others to guess. Ask the children why they think it is important to keep clean. What other things do people do to keep clean? Invite older children to make a poster about keeping clean to display in the group.

PAGE 11
NASTY OR NICE?

Learning objective
To show a range of feelings in response to experiences of the world. (Personal, Social and Emotional Development)
Group size
Small groups.

Cut out the pictures from a copy of the photocopiable sheet. Look at one picture at a time with the children and ask them to decide whether it shows something nasty or nice. Encourage all the children to participate and to talk about their personal experiences. Help younger children to elaborate by sensitively asking them questions. What did you do next? Who can help you when you are upset? Ask older children to think of happy endings for the 'nasty' pictures.

PAGE 12
MORNING, NOON AND NIGHT

Learning objectives
To talk about personal experiences; to sequence events. (Language and Literacy)
Group size
Up to four children.

Ensure that the children are familiar with the words 'morning', 'afternoon' and 'night'. Talk about the pictures on the photocopiable sheet using appropriate 'time' vocabulary such as before, next and after. Provide each child with a copy of the photocopiable sheet and let them cut out and sort the pictures into 'morning', 'afternoon' and 'night' as they relate their own experiences to the familiar scenes. Encourage the children to put the pictures in the order that they do things during the day. Let younger children choose two pictures to sequence, showing night and day.

Invite older children to share their picture sequences at circle time.

PAGE 13
THIS IS ME

Learning objective
To use pictures to communicate meaning. (Language and Literacy)
Group size
Up to five children.

Give each child a copy of the photocopiable sheet and show them how to fold it in half and half again to make a book (the front page should read, 'This is me'). Read the words together, pointing to each word as you say it.

Explain that you would like the children to draw pictures to match the words to make their own books. Encourage all the children to write their own names on the front page. Enlarge the sheet to A3 size for younger children who may find it hard to draw in the small spaces. Provide older children with extra paper to create additional pages.

PAGE 14
AT THE DOCTOR'S

Learning objective
To develop writing skills through role-play. (Language and Literacy)
Group size
Up to four children.

Develop your role-play area into a doctor's clinic or hospital. Over time, introduce a range of resources to maintain the children's interest. These could include uniforms; children's play medical kits; different types of bandages; injured toys; diary, pad and telephone for the receptionist; a shoebox turned into a filing box containing index cards.

The photocopiable sheet provides a template for a medical record card. Copy the sheet onto card and cut out a batch for use in the clinic. Go into role

with the children and show them how to fill out and use the medical record card during a doctor's consultation!

PAGE 15

BATHTIME

Learning objective
To tell a story and talk about personal experiences. (Language and Literacy)
Group size
Up to five children.

Share a book about bathtimes, such as *Mr Archimedes' Bath* by Pamela Allen (Puffin). Encourage the children to talk about their own bathtimes. Give each child a copy of the photocopiable sheet and talk about the pictures together. Ask the children to cut the pictures out and put them in the correct order. Invite each child to tell you the story, encouraging him/her to relate it to their own experiences. What toys do you play with in the bath? Do you sometimes have bubble bath?

Let younger children sequence just two or three of the pictures and encourage older children to draw what happens next.

PAGE 16

BIRTHDAY TEA

Learning objective
To solve a simple practical problem using one-to-one correspondence and matching skills. (Mathematics)
Group size
Small groups.

Give each child a copy of the photocopiable sheet (enlarged if possible). Explain that the two plates belong to two people who are at a party. Both people need to have exactly the same food on their plates. Ask the children to cut out the food pictures and give each person exactly the same. Encourage them to check to make sure.

Support younger children by handing them two of the same thing at a time and asking them to place one of each item on each plate. Ask older children to draw extra things for both people, making sure that both plates still have identical food.

PAGE 17

COUNT THE CANDLES

Give each child some Plasticine and ask them to make a small 'cake'. Provide some birthday candles, or objects of similar size such as pencils or cut-up straws, and give each child a number from 1 to 6. Ask them to count out that number of candles and put them into their Plasticine cake. Line up the cakes in order from 1 to 6. Now, give each child a copy of the photocopiable sheet and ask them to cut out the cakes, count the candles and then stick the pictures on a strip of paper in the right order from 1 to 6. Concentrate on the numbers 1 to 3 with younger children. Ask older children to write the numbers of candles inside the cakes.

Learning objective
To count and order numbers to six. (Mathematics)
Group size
Six children.

PAGE 18

FOR BABY AND ME

Talk with the children about growing up and share a book such as *The Baby's Catalogue* by Janet and Allan Ahlberg (Puffin). Give each child a copy of the photocopiable sheet and talk about the pictures. Ask the children to cut out the pictures and sort them into sets: one for baby and one for 'me'. Ask older children to draw extra pictures to add to the sets. Develop the idea further by creating a Venn diagram, showing things that both child and baby enjoy, such as milk and teddies.

Learning objective
To sort everyday objects. (Mathematics)
Group size
Up to six children.

PAGE 19

HANDS ON

Give each child a copy of the photocopiable sheet and ask them to draw around their hand inside the frame. Provide some objects such as a pencil, spatula and Lego brick. Let the children compare the objects to the length of their hand. Encourage them to use comparative vocabulary such as 'shorter than' or 'longer than'. Ask them to choose some objects to draw inside the appropriate boxes. Emphasize the practical parts of the activity with younger children and encourage them to draw just one thing in each box. Set

Learning objective
To use mathematical language to describe size. (Mathematics)
Group size
Small groups.

further challenges for older children, such as finding out how many Lego bricks long their hand is.

PAGE 20
MAKES SENSE

Use this activity to reinforce understanding of the five senses. Provide each child with a copy of the photoocopiable sheet. Show them how to cut out the book and fold it to make a zigzag book. Read the words together, asking the children to think of words to fill the gaps, such as 'I can smell flowers'. Let them draw a picture to match the words on each page. Younger children will need help to choose the words. Scribe their chosen word for them. Let older children attempt to write the missing words for themselves.

PAGE 21
ACROSS THE AGES

Cut out the pictures on the photocopiable sheet then encourage the children to talk about each one, relating them to people and events in their own lives. Do they know any babies? Do they remember any funny things that they did when they were a baby? As a group, decide on the order of age of the people and make an age timeline. Concentrate on the difference between young and old with younger children. Ask older children to make a simple timeline, showing themselves as a baby, a child, and how they imagine themselves as an adult.

PAGE 22
HANDS AND FEET

Enlarge a copy of the photocopiable sheet (if possible). Talk about what the pictures show with the children and in a space ask them to mime each of the actions in turn. After each one, ask them whether they used their hands or their feet the most. Give each child a sheet and ask them to draw an arrow between the activities and the appropriate body parts. Talk about the pictures on the sheet with younger children and guide them as they draw

their arrows. Encourage older children to mime other things that they use their hands or feet for.

PAGE 23
MAGIC CARPET

Give each child a copy of the photocopiable sheet and explain that you would like them to design their own magic carpet. Provide a selection of patterned fabric pieces and paint colour charts to give ideas. Ask them to practise copying their chosen pattern onto a piece of paper and help them to mix the paints to create their favourite colours. Encourage the children to decorate their carpets carefully. Let younger children choose from a selection of ready-mixed paints and collage materials. Encourage older children to fill in the sentence at the bottom of the sheet and to write a story about their carpet.

PAGE 24
TREASURE BOX

Make a treasure box from the template to show to the children. Place a tiny photograph or picture in it. Explain that treasures don't have to be valuable, just special. Show them your box and treasure. What things do the children treasure and why? Enlarge the photocopiable sheet to A3 size for each child. Help them to cut out and decorate it with collage materials, paints or crayons before you help them to stick it together with glue or sticky tape (younger children will need plenty of assistance). Let the children take their boxes home to use as treasure boxes.

Learning objective
To learn about the senses. (Knowledge and Understanding of the World)
Group size
Up to four children.

Learning objective
To talk about families and past and present events in own life. (Knowledge and Understanding of the World)
Group size
Small groups.

Learning objective
To move confidently and imaginatively in a controlled manner. (Physical Development)
Group size
Whole group.

Learning objective
To use imagination and explore colour and pattern. (Creative Development)
Group size
Up to six children.

Learning objective
To make a treasure box and to communicate feelings. (Creative Development)
Group size
Up to six children.

Keeping clean

◆ Talk about these pictures.

Nasty or nice?

◆ Talk about what's happening in each picture.

Morning, noon and night

◆ Cut out the pictures. Sort them into sets.

This is me

◆ Cut out and fold along the dotted lines.
Draw pictures to match the words.

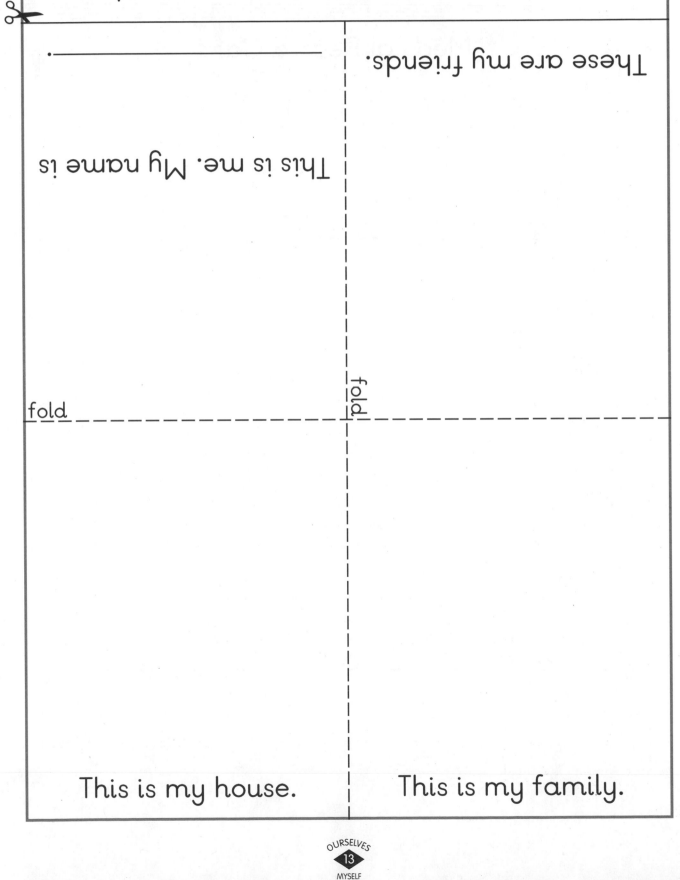

These are my friends.

This is me. My name is

fold

This is my house.

This is my family.

At the doctor's

◆ Use this card at the doctor's clinic.

Medical Record Card

Name _____

Birthday _____

Age _____

Symptoms _____

_____

_____

_____

Signed _____

Bathtime

◆ Cut out and colour the pictures. Put them in the correct order.

Birthday tea

◆ Cut out the food and stick the food onto the plates. Give both plates the same.

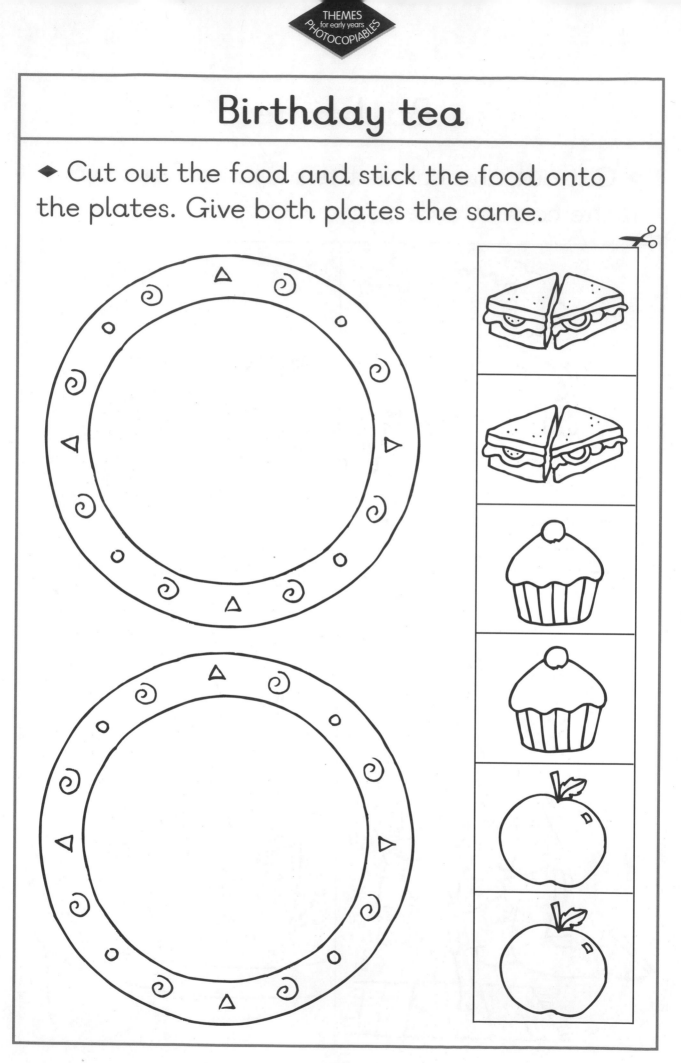

Count the candles

◆ Cut out the pictures. Count the candles
and put them in order.

For baby and me

◆ Cut out the pictures and sort them into two sets.

Hands on

◆ Draw around your hand. Now draw things that are shorter and longer than your hand.

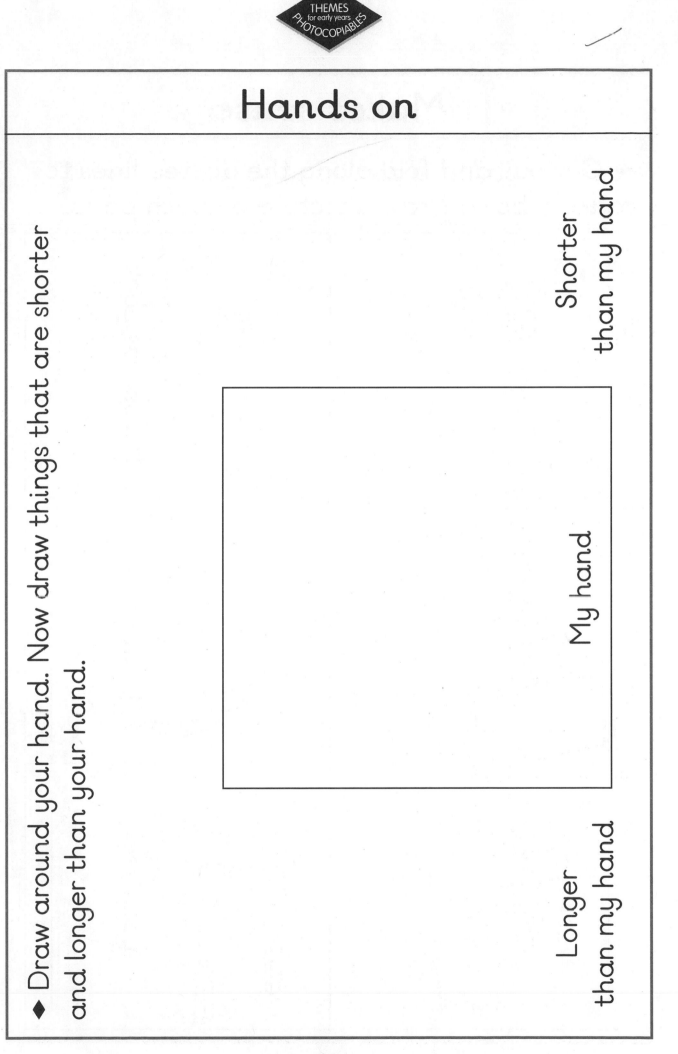

Shorter than my hand

My hand

Longer than my hand

Makes sense

◆ Cut out and fold along the dotted lines to make a book. Draw a picture on each page.

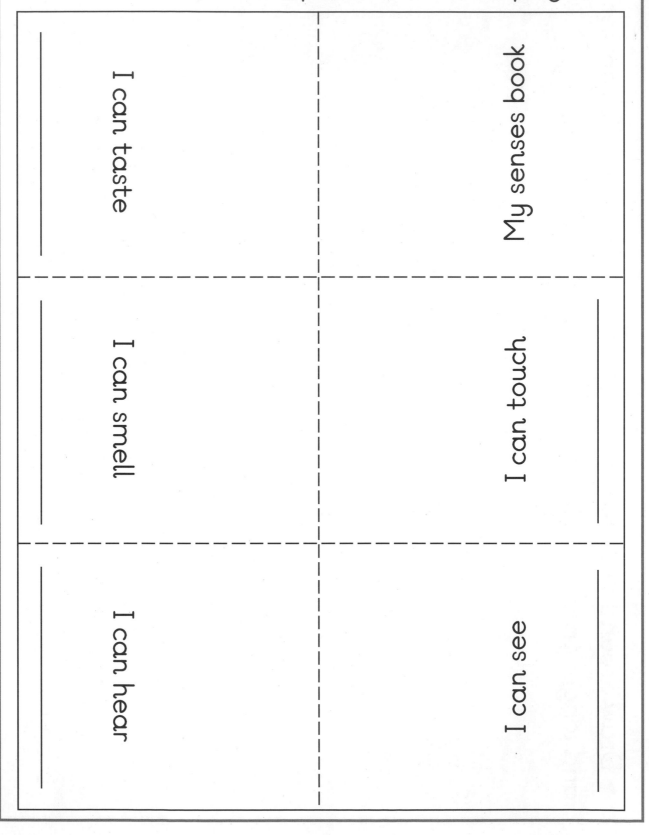

I can taste

My senses book

I can smell

I can touch

I can hear

I can see

Across the ages

◆ Cut out the pictures and put them in order of age.

Hands and feet

◆ Match the activity to the hands or the feet by drawing an arrow.

Magic carpet

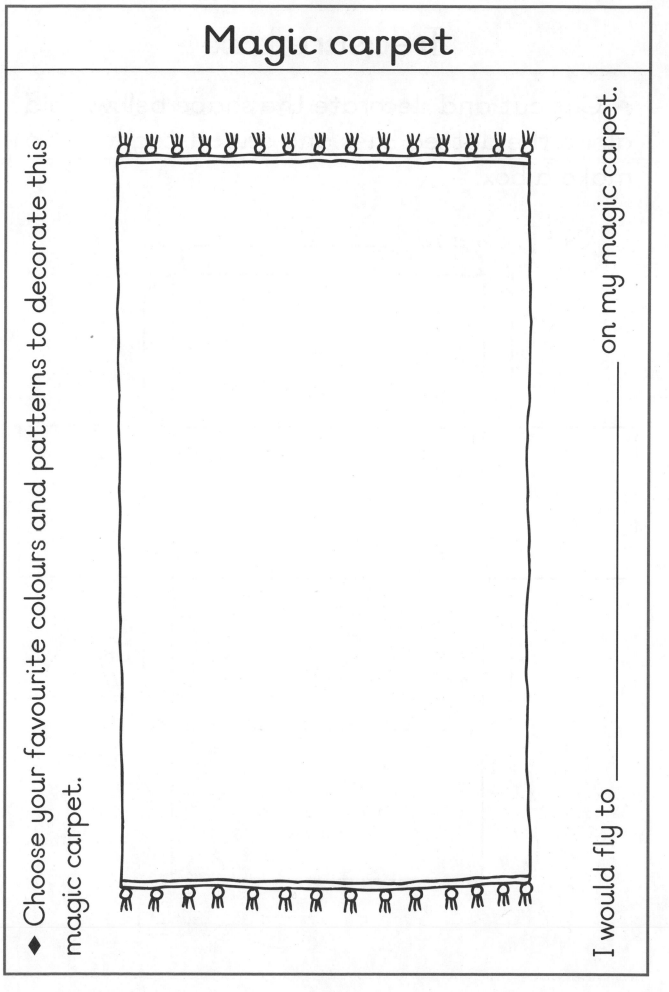

◆ Choose your favourite colours and patterns to decorate this magic carpet.

I would fly to _____ on my magic carpet.

Treasure box

◆ Cut out and decorate the shape below. Fold along the dotted lines and stick it together to make a box.

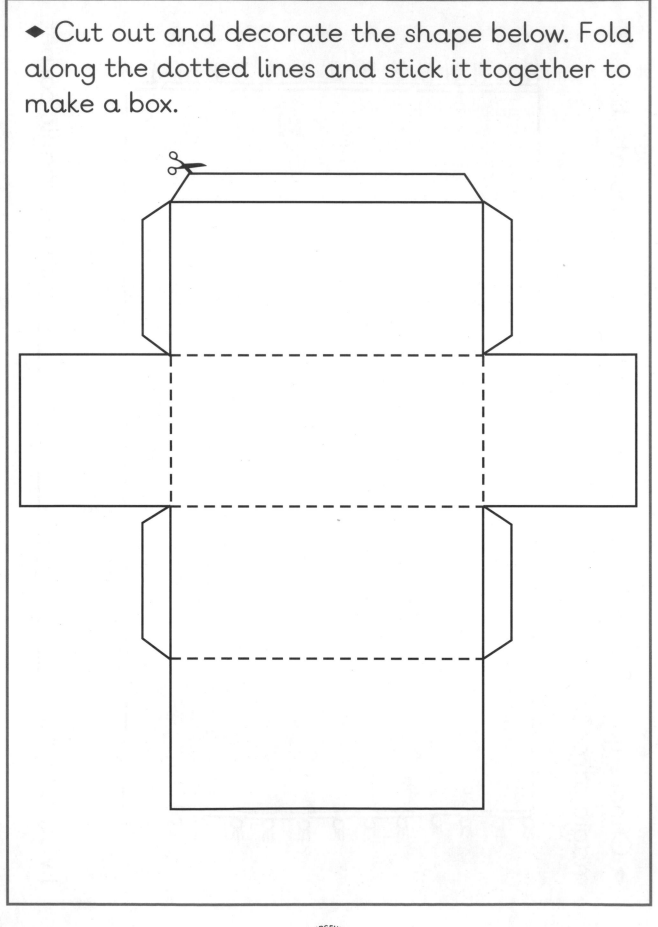

HOMES

PAGE 28
TIDY-UP TIME

Learning objective
To treat personal property with care and concern. (Personal, Social and Emotional Development)
Group size
Whole group.

Establish a group routine for tidying-up. Let a different child be the tidy-up inspector each day. They must make sure everything gets put away in the right place. Explain how we need to keep everything clean and tidy so that it can be used another day. Give each child a copy of the photocopiable sheet and explain that all the objects need to be put away – some in the wardrobe and some in the toy box. Ask the children to cut out the pictures and stick them in the correct place. Help younger children to decide where things go. Ask older children to help you write a list of tidy-up time rules.

PAGE 29
LETTER SEARCH

Learning objective
To recognize the letter 'b' by shape and sound. (Language and Literacy)
Group size
Whole group/ individuals.

Put some objects beginning with the letter sound 'b' into a feely bag and repeat the phrase: 'I begin with 'b', said the bear/ball/bead' as you bring out each object. Encourage the children to join in. Write the letter 'b' onto an easel, showing the children how to form it correctly. Give each child a copy of the photocopiable sheet and ask them to find and circle all the 'b' sounds in the bedroom. Simply talk about the picture with younger children, emphasizing all the 'b' sounds. Ask older children to write a list of the 'b' words on a sheet of paper.

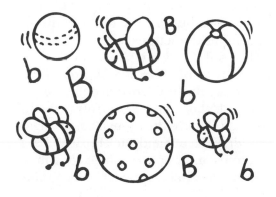

PAGE 30
OPEN-UP!

Learning objective
To use pictures to communicate meaning. (Language and Literacy)
Group size
Small groups.

Share some lift-the-flap books with the children, such as *What's inside?* by Eric Hill (Puffin). Give each child a photocopied sheet. Help them to cut out the pictures and stick one edge to a piece of paper to make 'flaps'. Encourage them to think of and draw some objects to go under each flap (such as butter and milk in the fridge). Help younger children to cut and stick their pictures. Let them hide just one thing under each flap. Encourage older children to make two more flaps of different pieces of furniture. Help them to make their pictures into a book.

PAGE 31
ANYONE IN?

Learning objective
To use pictures and familiar words to communicate meaning. (Language and Literacy)
Group size
Whole group/ individuals.

Encourage the children to talk about the people that live in their homes. Ask them to try to remember everyone, including pets! Give each child a copy of the photocopiable sheet, enlarged to A3 size. Show them how to cut and fold the shape to make a house. Ask them to draw all the people that live in their home inside the house. Write the people's names for younger children and encourage them to use comparative vocabulary such as oldest and youngest. Ask older children to draw the people in order of age and to write their names underneath.

PAGE 32
BUYING A HOUSE

Learning objective
To use writing in a role-play setting. (Language and Literacy)
Group size
Up to four children.

Develop your role-play area into an Estate Agent's. Include posters around the walls and create an office area with filing boxes, telephone, table, chairs and so on. Provide pictures of homes. Make several copies of the photocopiable sheet for the children to use. Go into role as an Estate Agent and show them how to fill in the details. Encourage the children to draw a property or cut out pictures to add to the sheet.

Encourage older children to describe the property in the 'notes' section. Invite younger children to draw their own home in the box. Ask them to tell you about their home and scribe their notes for them.

PAGE 33

COTTAGE IN THE WOODS

Learning objective
To use numbers in a practical counting game. (Mathematics)
Group size Pairs.

Enlarge the photocopiable sheet to A3 size, colour it in and laminate it. Tell the story of *Hansel and Gretel* (Traditional). Explain that in the game the children can help Hansel and Gretel to get safely home by following the pebbles in the moonlight. Give each child a counter. Show them how to throw the dice, count, and move along the pebbles. Provide a dice with 1 to 3 spots for younger children and help them to develop one-to-one correspondence by guiding their hand as they count the spaces. Make the game more difficult for older children by asking them to use two dice, and to add or subtract the totals that they throw.

PAGE 34

HOUSE SHAPES

Learning objective
To solve simple practical problems using knowledge of shapes. (Mathematics)
Group size Four children.

Make a shape dice (using sticky labels) to match the shapes shown on the photocopiable sheet. Give each child a copy of the sheet and ask them to take it in turns to throw the dice. Encourage them to say the name of the shape and then to cut out the same shape from their sheet. When they have cut out all their shapes, ask them to arrange and stick them onto a piece of paper to make a house. Enlarge the sheet and make one group picture with younger children. Ask older children to design some shape furniture for the house.

PAGE 35

NEXT TO THE BED...

Learning objective
To use positional language. (Mathematics)
Group size Pairs.

Ask the children to talk about their bedrooms. Can they describe where things are using words such as 'next to' and 'behind'? Give pairs of children a copy of the photocopiable sheet each and ask them to take it in turns to cut out the objects and arrange them in the bedroom. Let them sit opposite each other with a screen between them. Tell the first child to give his partner instructions for placing the objects in the same places as his own. Compare the finished rooms. Which things are the same/different? Swap over roles. Let younger children work individually. Encourage them to describe where they have placed the objects.

PAGE 36

HOUSE NUMBERS

Learning objective
To sequence and count using familiar objects. (Mathematics)
Group size Whole group.

Give six children a number card each from 1 to 6. Ask them to hold up their numbers and stand in order. Count out loud. Ask the other children to close their eyes as you remove one of the 'numbers'. Which number is missing? Where should it go? Repeat and vary the game. Give each child a copy of the photocopiable sheet and ask them to fill in the missing numbers. The third row has been left blank – use it to reflect your current work (odds and evens; numbers to 20 and so on). With younger children, practise counting the houses and make a simple 1 to 5 number line (replace the existing numbers).

PAGE 37

WHICH ROOM?

Learning objective
To develop matching skills using everyday objects and events. (Mathematics)
Group size Small groups.

Look at the pictures on the photocopiable sheet with the children and mime the actions together, singing, 'This is the way we clean our teeth...' to the tune of 'Here We Go Round the Mulberry Bush'. Give each child a sheet and ask them to draw arrows to join the activities to the rooms. Let younger children cut out and stick the matching pictures onto separate sheets of paper, adding any relevant pictures of their

own. Ask older children to choose another room and make a list of the things that they do there.

PAGE 38
SMALL WORLD

Learning objective
To develop an awareness of the local environment. (Knowledge and Understanding of the World)
Group size
Pairs.

Enlarge the photocopiable sheet to A3 size and give each pair of children a copy. Ask them to colour it in carefully, using appropriate colours for the roads, trees and buildings. Laminate their finished designs and encourage them to play together, using small vehicles and construction materials to make houses and other buildings. Pre-prepare some playmats for younger children to use. Let older children add additional sections to their playmats. Encourage them to relate their playmats to the local area, using relevant vocabulary to describe the roads, bridges, houses and vehicles.

PAGE 39
ALL SORTS OF HOMES

Learning objective
To learn about the features of different types of homes. (Knowledge and Understanding of the World)
Group size
Whole group.

Enlarge a copy of the photocopiable sheet and display it on an easel so that all the children can see it. At circle time, invite the children to take it in turns to talk about one of the pictures. It might be about their own home, a day trip to see a castle, or a holiday in a caravan. Add extra detail to the children's contributions and ask them questions such as: What is this home made of? How old do you think it is? Is it bigger or smaller than your home?

PAGE 40
LENDING A HAND

Learning objective
To move with confidence and imagination. (Physical Development)
Group size
Whole group.

Look at an A3 size copy of the photocopiable sheet together. What is the person doing in each picture? In a large space, ask the children to mime each of the actions in turn. Encourage them to use their whole bodies as they make the actions; stretching high, bending low, twisting and twirling. Play some music with different tempos (such as Grieg's 'Morning' suite from *Peer Gynt*) and encourage the children to mime their cleaning actions as they dance to the music.

For younger children, concentrate on just one or two of the actions.

PAGE 41
NOTICE-BOARD

Learning objective
To take part in imaginative play. (Creative Development)
Group size
Up to four children.

Set up your role-play area into a traditional home corner. Go into role with the children and provide them with ideas for their play, such as suggesting that they invite some friends to tea. Put up a notice-board and encourage them to use it to stick up postcards, shopping lists, invitations and so on. Make several copies of the photocopiable sheet and show the children how to fill out the shopping lists and reminders. Encourage younger children to use scribbles or play-writing. Over time, you will notice the emergence of recognizable letter-shapes in their writing.

PAGE 42
THROUGH THE WINDOW

Learning objective
To develop imagination through a simple art activity. (Creative Development)
Group size
Small groups.

Begin by reading the story *Through My Window* by Tony Bradman (Little Mammoth) to the children. Ask them to tell you what they can see through their bedroom window at home. What would the children like to see if they could choose? Give each child a copy of the photocopiable sheet and ask them to draw a picture of something that they would like to see.

Help younger children to think of a place to draw by asking questions, such as: Where do you like to go? What can you do there? Encourage older children to make a lift-the-flap picture, by drawing curtains to stick over the top of their pictures.

Tidy-up time

◆ Cut out the pictures and tidy them in the right place.

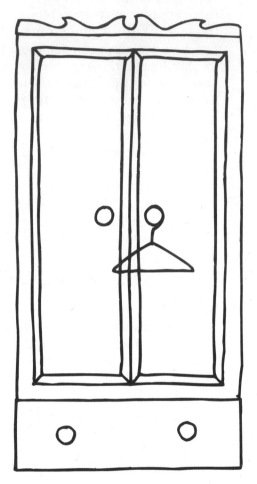

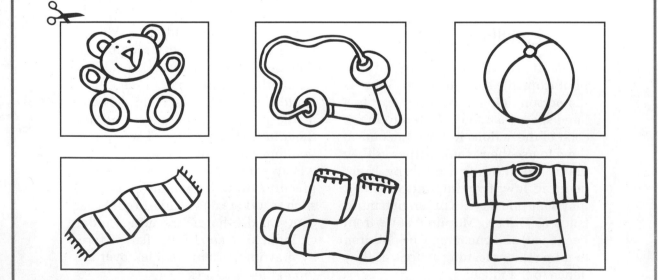

Letter search

◆ Draw a circle around all the things beginning with b .

Open-up!

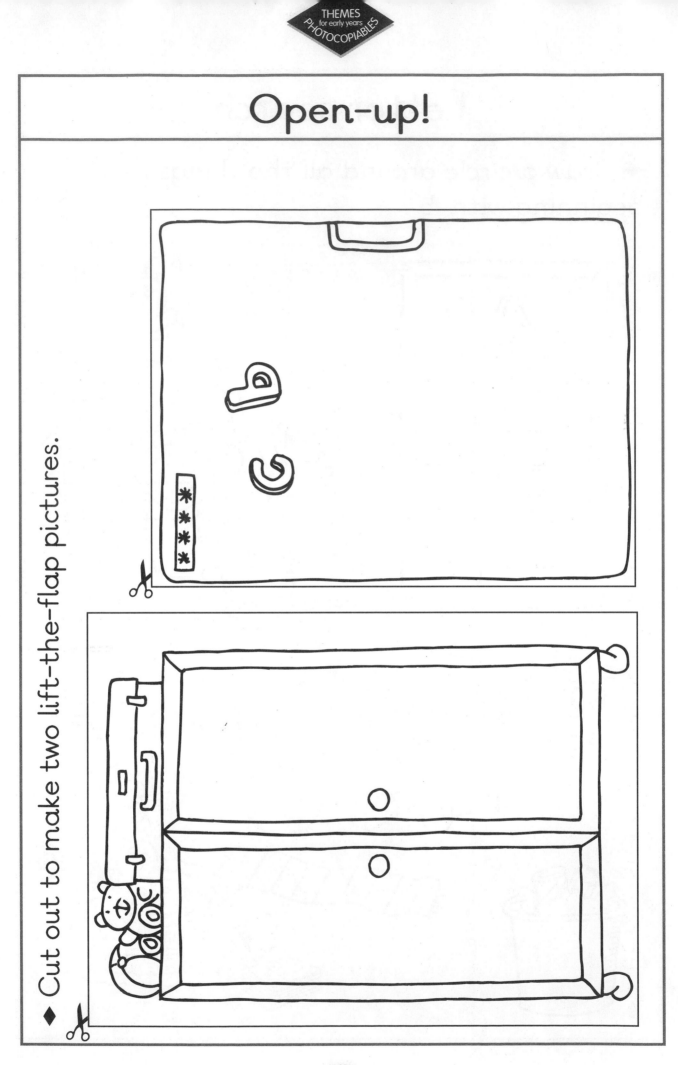

◆ Cut out to make two lift-the-flap pictures.

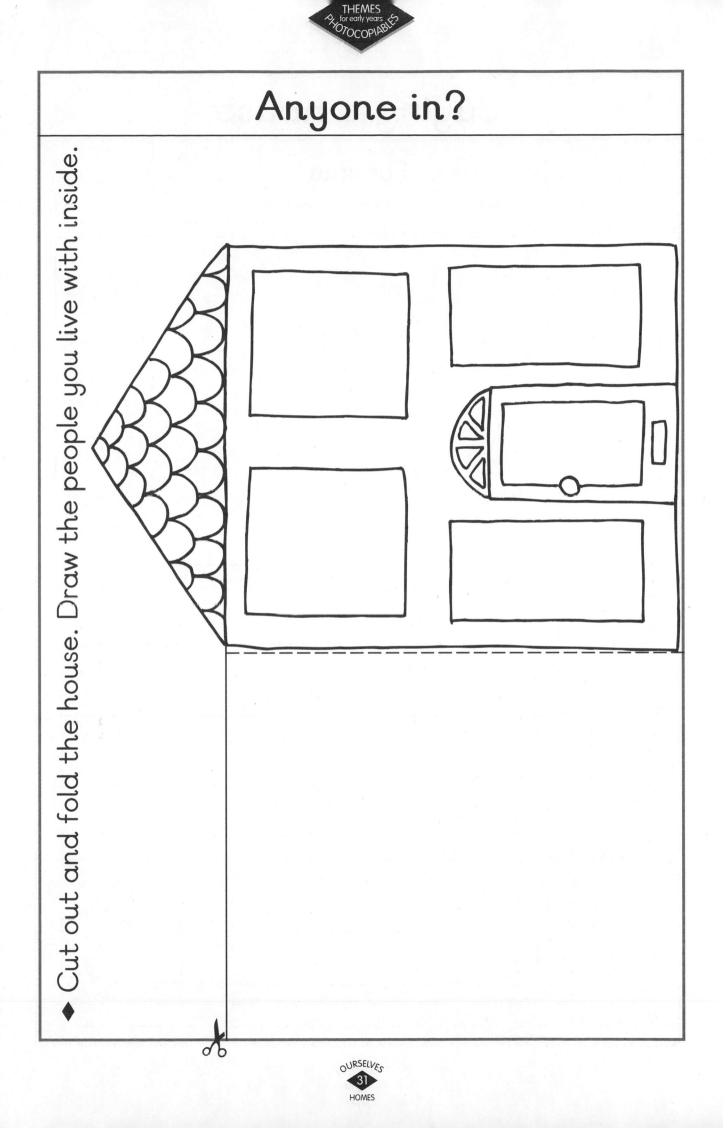

Anyone in?

◆ Cut out and fold the house. Draw the people you live with inside.

Buying a house

For sale

Type of home _____

Price £ _____

Number of rooms _____

Town/village _____

Notes _____

_____

Cottage in the woods

House shapes

◆ Cut out the shapes. Arrange them to make a house.

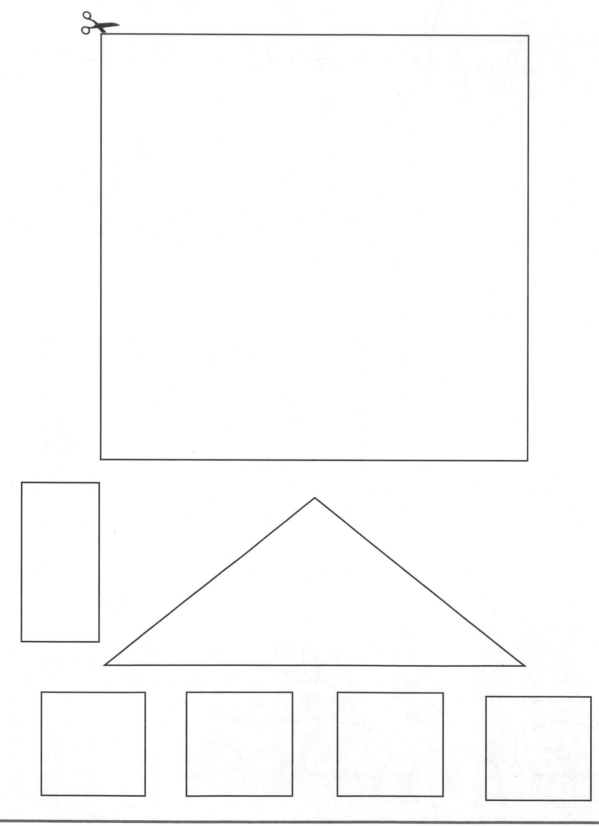

Next to the bed

◆ Cut out the pictures and arrange them in the bedroom.

House numbers

◆ Fill in the missing numbers.

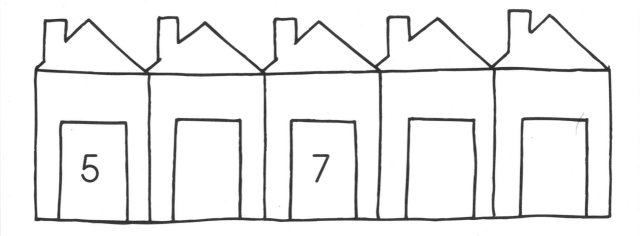

Which room?

◆ Draw arrows to the correct rooms.

Small world

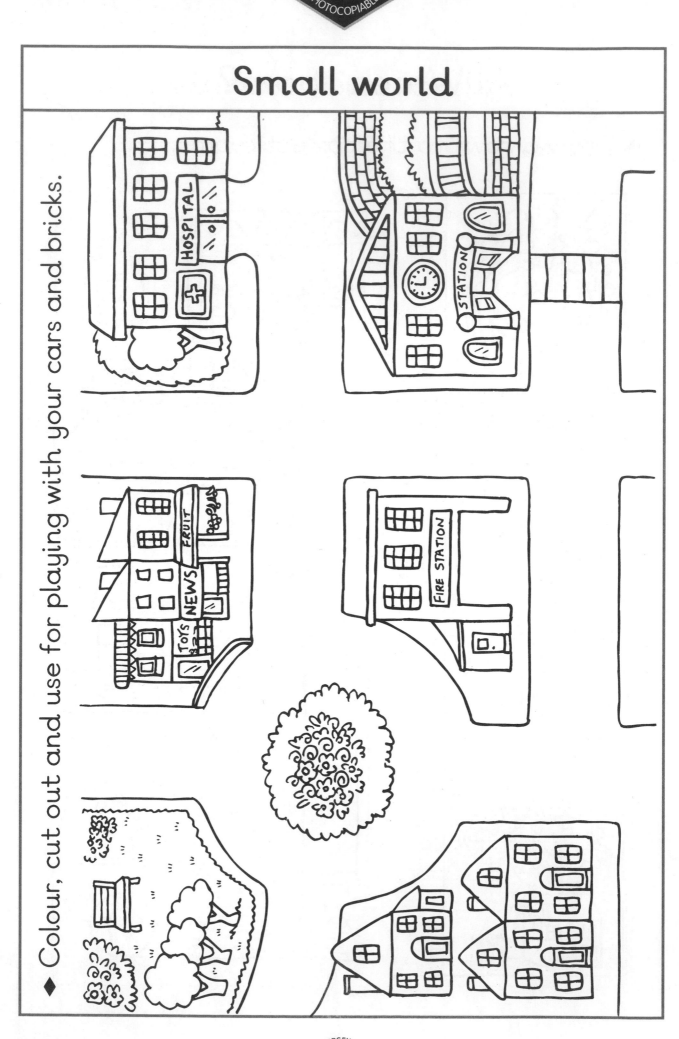

◆ Colour, cut out and use for playing with your cars and bricks.

All sorts of homes

◆ Talk about the different homes.

Lending a hand

◆ Mime the actions in the pictures.

Notice-board

Reminders

Shopping list

◆ Use these pieces of paper in the home corner.

Through the window

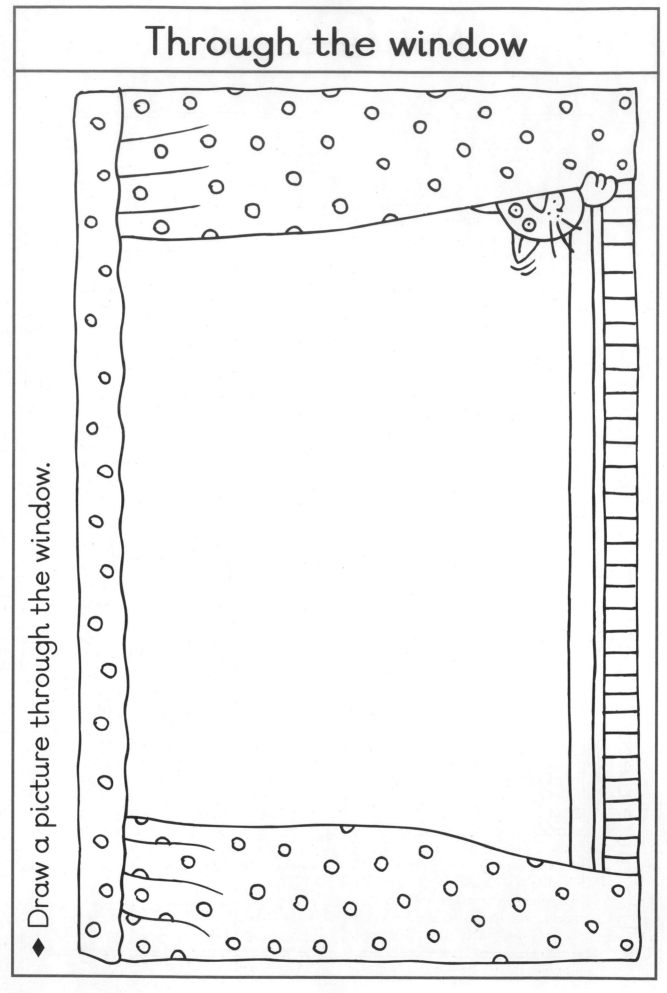

◆ Draw a picture through the window.

TOYS

PAGE 46

SHARE THE TOYS

earning objective
o learn how o share fairly. Personal, ocial and motional Development) Group size Whole group.

During circle time, talk to the children about sharing with each other. Ask them to tell you about a time when they played nicely with someone else and shared the toys together. Why is it important to share out the toys? Give each child a copy of the photocopiable sheet and ask them to draw arrows between the toys and the children, making sure that each child has the same things.

PAGE 47

TOY MATCH

earning objectives
o take turns and share fairly; o work with a partner. Personal, ocial and motional Development) Group size Pairs.

Enlarge the photocopiable sheet to A3 size. Colour and cut out the dice template. Fold and stick together (encourage the children to help each other to hold the cube in place). In pairs, ask the children to throw the dice and match the pictures on the dice with those on the board, covering the pictures with their own coloured counters as they are matched. The emphasis of the activity is on taking turns and working closely with a partner. Allow younger children to colour the pictures on the dice, but construct it for them. Ask older children, working in pairs, to colour the dice and board pictures identically.

PAGE 48

TRAFFIC CONTROL

Learning objective
To use pictures and symbols to communicate meaning. (Language and Literacy) Group size Small groups.

Go for a walk in your local area to look for signs such as road signs, street names and so on. Back in your group, talk about the signs you have seen and try to think of some for the outdoor play area, such as 'slow down' and 'no throwing sand'. Give each child a copy of the photocopiable sheet. Talk about the sign shown and ask them to make up one of their own. Enlarge some of the children's signs, stick them to card and fix to a piece of dowelling. Let older children take it in turns to be traffic monitors, using the signs in the outdoor play area.

PAGE 49

TEDDY SURPRISE

Learning objective
To understand how books are organized and to use pictures, words and letters to convey meaning. (Language and Literacy) Group size Four children.

Help the children to cut out and fold the photocopiable sheet into a zigzag style book. Talk about the picture shapes together then ask them to pretend that they are walking up the stairs and going into their bedroom. How do they feel? What can they see? What happens when they open the door? Let older children have a go at writing the words to their surprise story and scribe the story for younger children. Younger children will also need help to cut out and fold the book.

PAGE 50

SANTA'S TOY FACTORY

Learning objective
To write for a specific purpose. (Language and Literacy) Group size Four children.

Develop your role-play area into Santa's toy factory. Decorate the walls with toy posters/drawings; provide tables with art, junk and collage materials. Make a simple toy with the children and show them how to fill in the instructions on the photocopiable sheet – drawing the things that they used in the boxes and the finished toy at the bottom. Talk through the order of making the toy with the children, scribing for younger children and encouraging older children to try to write their own words. Leave extra copies of the photocopiable sheet in the factory for the children to use whenever they have made something.

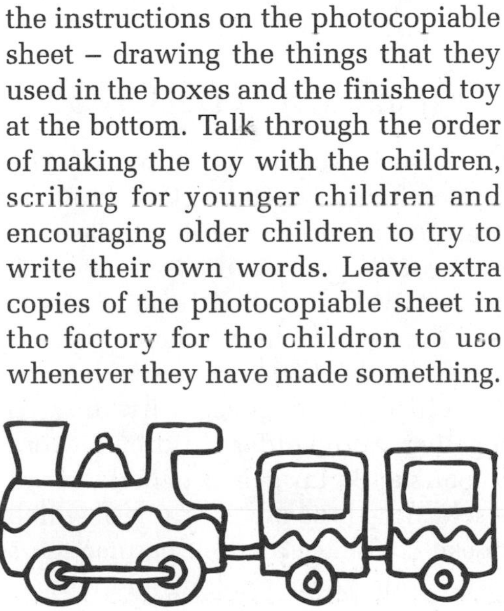

PAGE 51

ON THE BUS

Enlarge the photocopiable sheet, then colour and cut out the buses. Ask each child in turn to count out a number of play people and put them on a bus. How many are on the top floor? How many are on the bottom? How many altogether? Say, for example: 'Three people on the top and two on the bottom makes five people altogether'. Use the photocopiable sheet in the following ways, depending on ability:
• counting and matching – put the same number of people on each bus
• number bonds work – split the same number of passengers (between floors) in as many ways as possible
• odd and even numbers – which numbers can be shared equally?

PAGE 52

TIDY THE TOYS

Give each child a copy of the photocopiable sheet and ask them to cut out the toys and put them in order from 1 to 6. Put a box in the middle of the table. Take turns to throw the dice, counting the dots and matching to a toy, if possible. If the throw matches, let them put the toy in the toy box. At the end of the game, sort the toys into number sets. Concentrate on the numbers to 3 with younger children. Extend the activity by changing the numbers to 7 to 12, use two dice and add them together.

PAGE 53

WHERE DO I BELONG?

Give each child a copy of the photocopiable sheet and talk about the pictures together. What are the toys made of? Where would you play with them? Ask the children to make specific sets, such as 'outside toys' or 'toy animals'. Make some sets and ask the children to guess why they go together. Invite older children to work in pairs and play games of odd one out – selecting three pictures, one of which doesn't belong. Can their partner guess which one doesn't belong and why?

PAGE 54

TEDDY SNAP

Give each child a copy of the photocopiable sheet and ask them to cut out the cards and put them in order from 0 to 8. Play some games with the cards, such as:
• shuffling the cards around and asking children to reorder them
• removing a card and asking the children to tell you which one is missing – where does it go?
• matching the teddy to a number symbol – ask the children to write the number on the back of the card.

Concentrate on the numbers to five with younger children. Help older children, in pairs, to use two sets of cards and play games of *Pelmanism* or *Number Snap*.

PAGE 55

TOYS AROUND THE WORLD

If possible, enlarge a copy of the photocopiable sheet. Cut out the pictures and talk about each one in turn. Tell the children that these pictures show children from different parts of the world playing with their toys. (The pictures show: USA; Namibia; Russia and Zambia.) What are the children in the pictures doing? What are the toys made of? What things are the same or different about the children's own toys and games? Ask older children to draw a picture of themselves playing with their favourite toy to add to the set.

Learning objective
To handle malleable materials with increasing control. (Physical Development)
Group size Small groups.

Learning objective
To handle construction materials with increasing control. (Physical Development)
Group size Up to four children.

Learning objective
To develop control when handling tools and materials. (Physical Development)
Group size Small groups.

PAGE 56
DOLLS' TEA PARTY

Set up a dolls' tea party with a doll, plate and cup for each child. Explain that you would like each child to make the food for the dolls' tea party. Give each child a copy of the photocopiable sheet and 'read' it together, looking at the words and the pictures. Now ask each child to use Plasticine or play dough to make the things on the menu. Let younger children choose two or three things to make. Ask older children to ensure that each doll is given the same amount of food.

PAGE 57
MAKE THE MODEL

Enlarge the photocopiable sheet to A3 size and copy onto card. Cut out the pictures and talk about each one in turn with a small group of children. What do they think the models are made from? Ask them to identify the shapes and sizes of the pieces used. Invite the children to choose one of the cards and try to copy the picture using building bricks or Lego.

Give younger children the simple bridge to copy. Ask older children to make a model of their choice and draw it onto a card to add to the set.

PAGE 58
AT THE FACTORY

You may like to complete this activity in conjunction with 'Santa's toy factory' (page 43). Give each child a copy of the photocopiable sheet and help them to cut out all the pieces. Ask the children to decorate the pieces before they fix them together using split pins (with adult help). Fasten the pins loosely so that the children can move the arms and legs of their robot. Enlarge the sheet for younger children and help them to cut out the pieces carefully. Fix the split pins for them, then show them how to move the joints afterwards.

PAGE 59
JACK-IN-THE-BOX

Begin the activity by showing the children a real Jack-in-the-box and ask them to pretend they are 'Jack', by crouching low and springing up when you clap! Enlarge the photocopiable sheet and help each child to assemble their box, using sticky tape to fix it in place. To make 'Jack', cut out the two long strips and colour each one a different colour. Stick the strips together in an 'L' shape and fold each strip over the other alternately (below). Fix down the ends with glue. Stick Jack's head onto the top of the 'spring' and secure inside the box.

Provide ready-made boxes for younger children and make a simple fan-style concertina, using just one strip of paper.

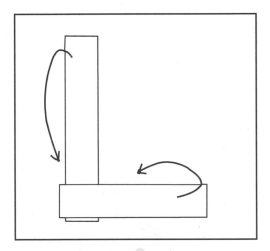

PAGE 60
THE THREE BEARS

Tell the children the story of *Goldilocks and the Three Bears* (Traditional). Enlarge the photocopiable sheet and cut out the characters then stick them onto card. Stick the picture onto a board. Assign a character to each child and ask them to colour it in and attach it to a piece of doweling using sticky tape. Let the children colour in the storyboard. Ask older children to use the puppets to act out the story as you retell it, encouraging them to say the repetitive phrases for their own character. Let younger children play freely with the stick puppets and the board.

Learning objective
To explore colour, texture and shape in three dimensions. (Creative Development)
Group size Up to four children.

Learning objective
To use a visual aid and imagination to retell a story. (Creative Development)
Group size Four children.

Share the toys

◆ Draw arrows from the toys to the children. Give each child the same.

Toy match

◆ Throw the dice and match the pictures.
Cover the pictures with a counter.

◆ Cut out and stick together to make a dice.

Traffic control

◆ Cut out and colour. Draw your own sign.

Teddy surprise

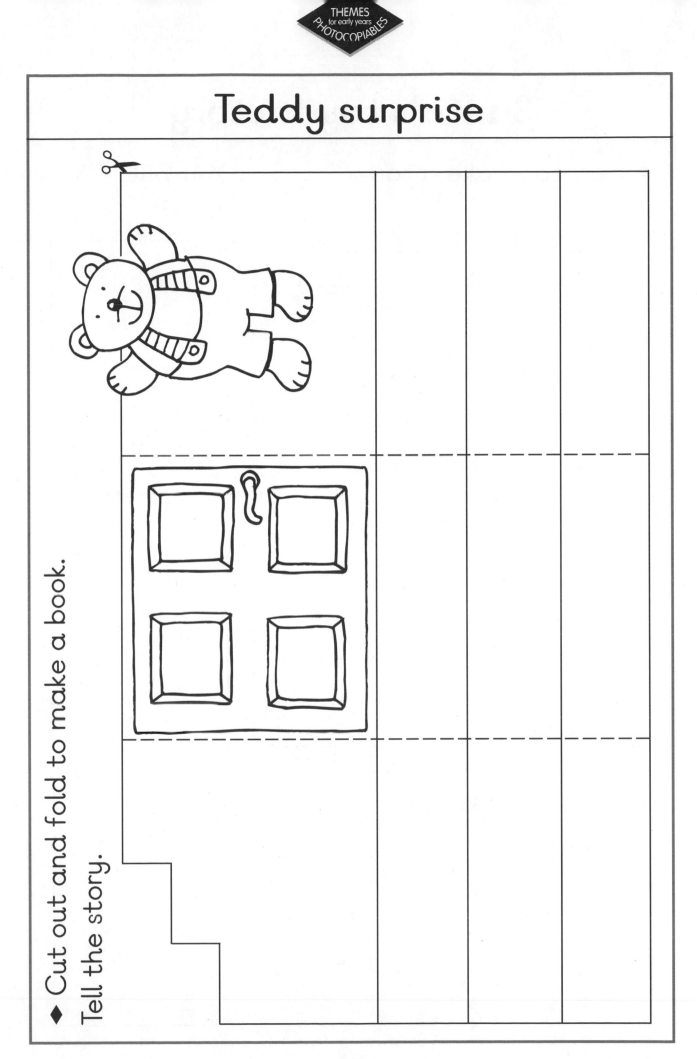

♦ Cut out and fold to make a book.

Tell the story.

Santa's toy factory

◆ How to make a toy

You will need:

It will look like this...

On the bus

◆ Draw __9__ passengers in each bus.

Tidy the toys

◆ Throw a dice and count the dots.
Cut out the matching toy and tidy it away.

Where do I belong?

◆ Cut out the toys and put them into sets.

Teddy snap

◆ Cut out the cards to play some games.

Toys around the world

◆ Talk about these pictures.

Dolls' tea party

◆ Make the things on the menu.

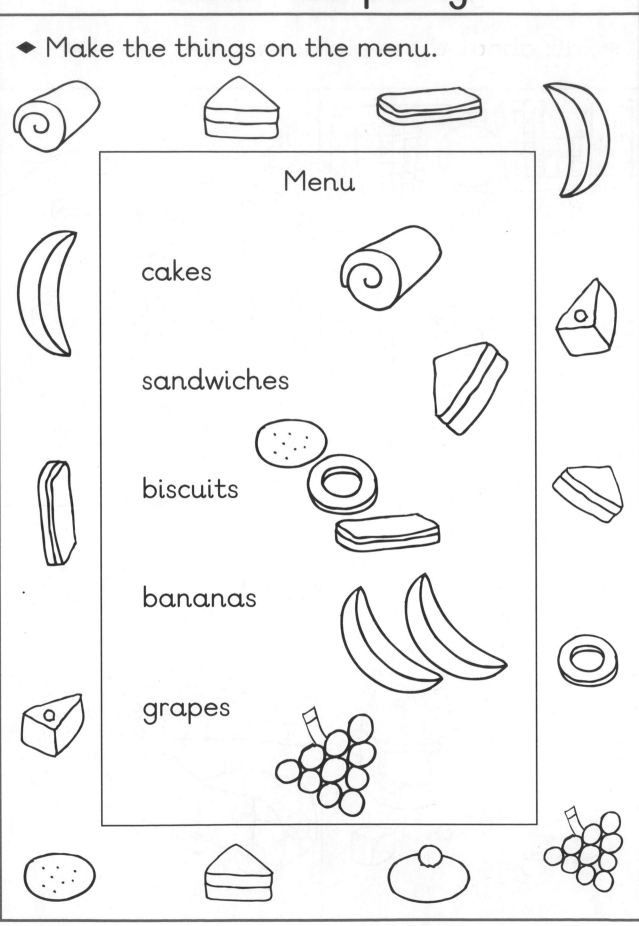

Menu

cakes

sandwiches

biscuits

bananas

grapes

Make the model

◆ Try to make these models.

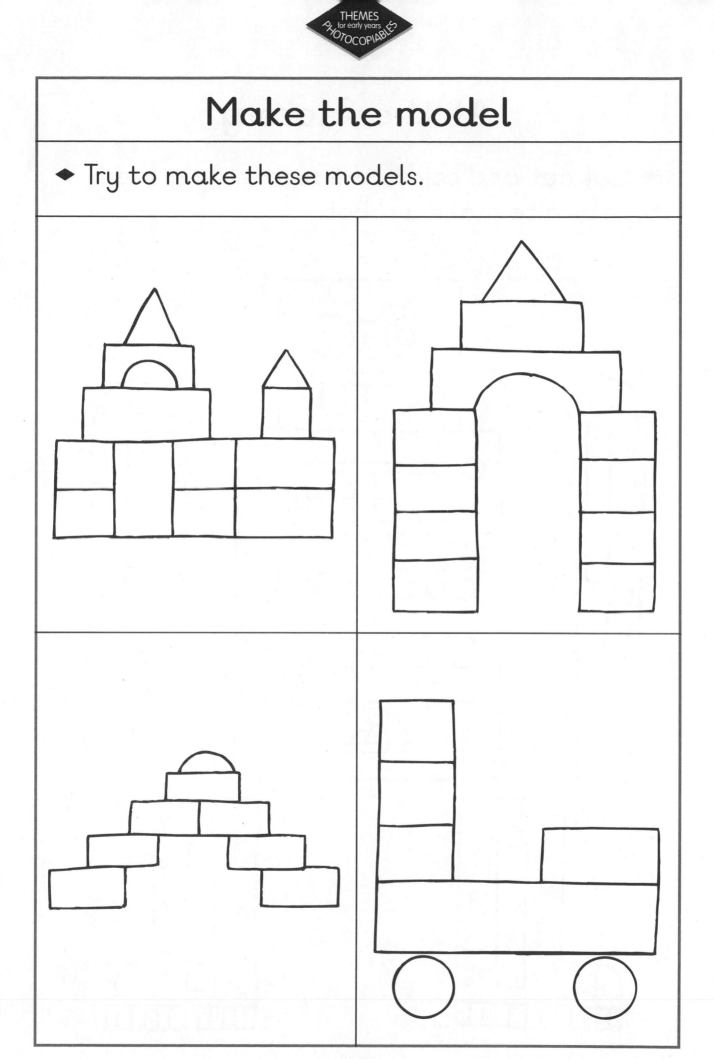

At the factory

◆ Cut out and colour the pieces. Join them together to make a robot.

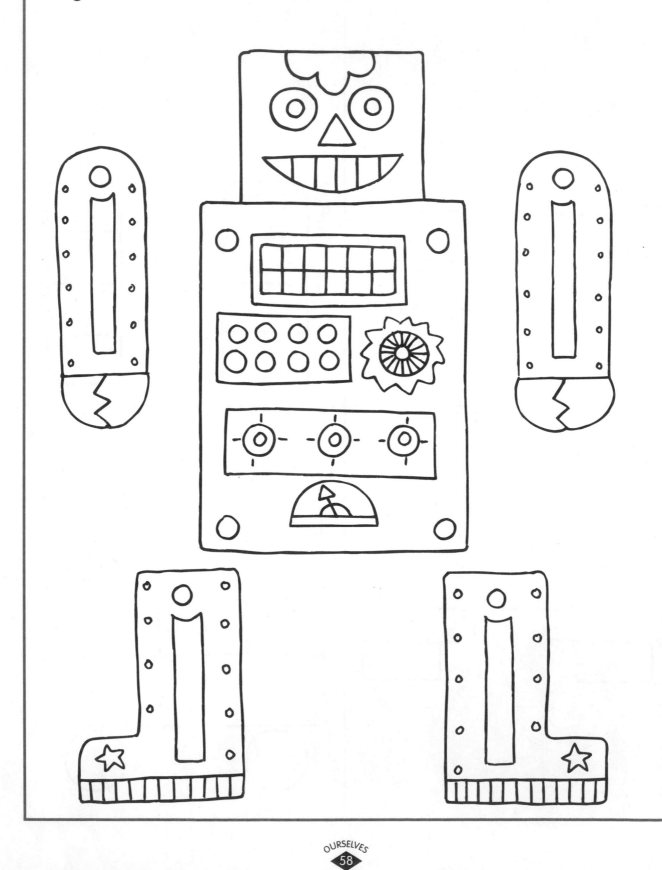

Jack-in-the-box

◆ Cut out and stick to make a Jack-in-the-box.

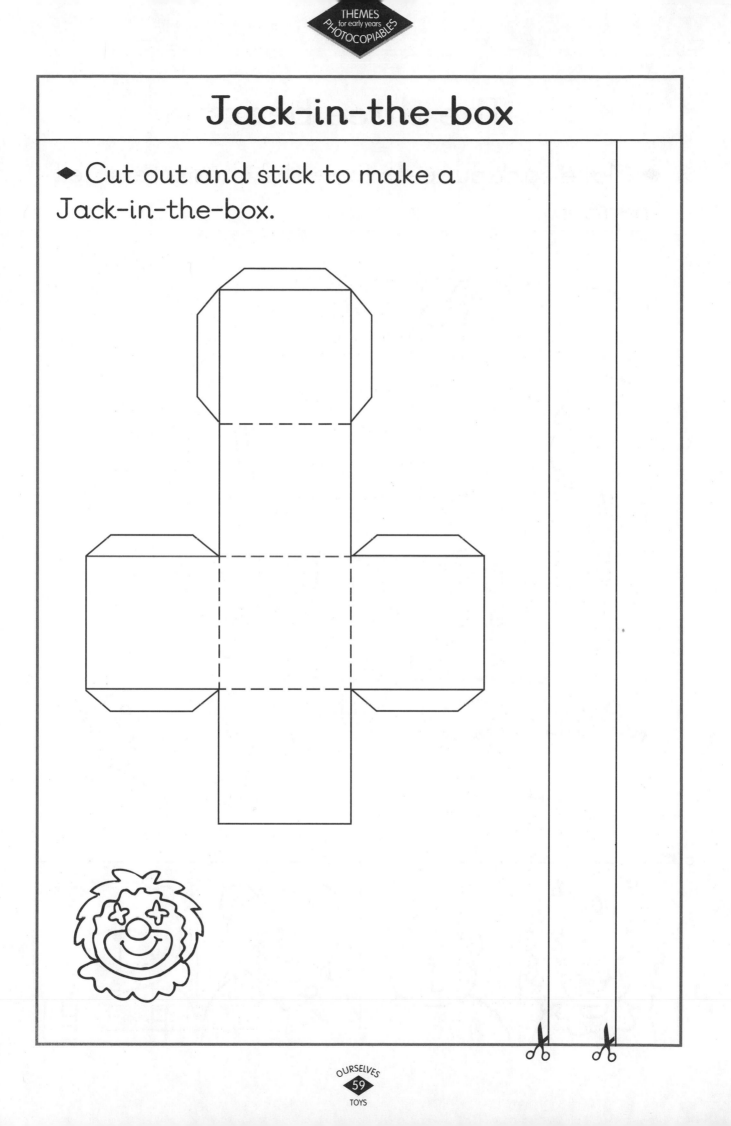

The three bears

◆ Make stick puppets from the characters. Tell the story.

CLOTHES

SPECIAL CLOTHES

Learning objective
To learn about a range of cultures and traditions. (Personal, Social and Emotional Development)
Group size
Whole group.

Enlarge a copy of the photocopiable sheet and cut out the pictures. Show the children the pictures, one at a time. Tell them a little bit about each one and invite them to add extra information. Perhaps they have been to a wedding recently, or perhaps they have been to see a football match. Explain that all the pictures show people dressed in special clothes. What special clothes do the children have? Encourage them to talk about their own experiences.

I CAN...

Learning objective
To encourage independence in getting dressed. (Personal, Social and Emotional Development)
Group size
Individuals.

Keep a copy of the photocopiable sheet in each child's personal record folder and let them colour in the stripes on the jumper when they have made significant achievements in getting dressed. Write the dates of their achievements on the back of the sheet as a record. When they have coloured in all the stripes, add a sentence to say 'I can dress myself'. Praise the children for their progress and let them finish colouring in the whole jumper.

COLOUR THE CLOTHES

Ask each child in turn to say the name and the letter sound of one of the things that they are wearing. Can they find the matching letter on an alphabet chart?

Give each child a copy of the photocopiable sheet and ask them to say the names of the clothes. Which ones begin with the same letter? Ask them to draw arrows to match up the two sets of clothes. Let them colour each pair in the same colour. Ask older children to think of another two items of clothing that begin with the same letter sound.

Learning objective
To group sets of clothes based on their letter sounds. (Language and Literacy)
Group size
Up to six children.

GETTING DRESSED

Ask the children to tell you about what they do when they get dressed in the morning. What things do they put on first? What things do they leave until last? How much help do the children need to get dressed?

Give each child a copy of the photocopiable sheet and ask them to cut out the pictures. As a group, talk about each of the pictures and decide on the correct order in which to put them. Encourage the children to relate the pictures to their own experience. Ask older children to add an extra picture or two to the sequence.

Learning objective
To retell and sequence a story. (Language and Literacy)
Group size
Small groups.

DESIGNER T-SHIRTS

Use the photocopiable sheet to practise pencil control and early writing patterns. Show the children the patterns on the sheet. Sit beside the child and practise drawing the patterns with your finger in the air and on the table before making marks on the sheet. When the child feels confident

Learning objective
To develop pencil control and early writing skills. (Language and Literacy)
Group size
Individuals.

enough to try to draw the pattern, give them a copy of the photocopiable sheet and help them to complete the patterns on the T-shirts.

Enlarge the sheet for younger children. Draw another blank T-shirt shape for older children and ask them to make up their own pattern.

PAGE 69
PRICE IT UP

Learning objective
To use writing in a role-play context. (Language and Literacy)
Group size
Up to four children.

Set up your role-play area as a clothes shop. Hang some clothes on a rail and attach price tags. Provide unbreakable mirrors, clothing catalogues, a till, posters and a 'Bargain box' of clothes and shoes for the children to sort. Invite the children to draw fashion advertisements and posters. Assign roles as customers and sales assistants and introduce scenarios such as shopping for a party outfit or for holiday clothes. Use the photocopiable sheet as a template for the children's play. It provides a price tag and price list. The children can add prices to the pictures and there is space for them to add an item.

PAGE 70
BEAUTIFUL BEADS

Learning objective
To recognize and recreate patterns. (Mathematics)
Group size
Up to six children.

Show the children a selection of beaded necklaces and talk about the shapes, colours and patterns. Identify the repeating patterns and cover a bead in your hand, asking the children to tell you what colour, shape or size of bead you are hiding.

Give each child a copy of the photocopiable sheet. Ask the children to tell you what the patterns are. Invite them to draw the rest of the pattern onto the sheet. With younger children, concentrate on simple colour patterns. Colour the beads in a repeating sequence and ask them to say the colour pattern. Encourage older children to make more complicated patterns including two attributes such as shape and size.

PAGE 71
SPOTS ON BOW TIES

The photocopiable sheet shows four bow ties for the children to add spots to, according to the chosen number. It may be used in a variety of ways:
• as a game – the children throw a dice and record their throw by drawing the same number of spots on the bow tie
• to practise counting skills – each bow tie has a different number of spots for the children to count (for younger children)
• to teach number bonds – older children have to arrange five dots on the two sides of the bow tie, making each bow tie different.

Learning objective
To develop knowledge of number bonds through a practical activity (Mathematics)
Group size
Small groups.

PAGE 72
OUR SHOES

During circle time, ask the children to tell you if they are wearing shorts, trousers or a skirt. Record the data in a block graph on an easel or board, using the photocopiable sheet as a guide. Use the graph for counting, comparing, ordering and sequencing work.

Now, work with small groups of children and help them to find out about each other's shoes. Help one child at a time to say the type of shoe that they are wearing and to colour in a square in the correct column. Talk about the results together.

Learning objective
To collect information and use it to develop comparing, ordering, sequencing and counting skills (Mathematics)
Group size
Whole group, small groups.

PAGE 73
RAIN OR SHINE?

As part of your regular routine, monitor the weather with the children. Make a chart using weather symbols that you change daily. Talk to the children about the clothes they wear in different kinds of weather. What sort of shoes are good for hot/rainy/cold weather?

Give each child a copy of the photocopiable sheet and talk about the weather symbols. Look at the pictures and ask the children to decide whether they would be good things to wear if it was rainy or sunny. Ask them to draw arrows between the clothes and the weather symbols to match them up.

Learning objective
To use knowledge of weather characteristics to solve simple problems (Knowledge and Understanding of the World)
Group size
Small groups.

PAGE 74
CLOTHES TIMELINE

Learning objective
To understand how people change as they grow older. (Knowledge and Understanding of the World)
Group size
Six children.

Enlarge the photocopiable sheet to A3 size. Cut out the pictures and talk about each one with the children. What clothes are the people wearing? What sort of things do babies wear? What would be different about a baby's shoes and a grown-up's shoes?

Give each child in the group a picture and ask them to take turns to put their picture down in the correct order to make a timeline from baby to grown-up. Let younger children sequence just three of the pictures, showing baby, child and grown-up. Invite older children to draw a picture of themselves to add to the timeline.

PAGE 75
LACE IT UP

Learning objective
To develop control and co-ordination. (Physical Development)
Group size
Small groups.

Enlarge the photocopiable sheet to A3 size and either copy or glue it onto card. Use a hole punch to punch out the holes as marked. Provide each child with a thick, blunt tapestry needle and thread or wool. Help them to thread the needle and then show them how to sew in and out of the holes on the trousers. The children will be developing their fine motor skills as they thread the pattern onto the trousers.

Invite older children to draw some different clothes onto card and punch holes in the pictures for them to do some more threading.

PAGE 76
JEWELLERY GEMS

Learning objective
To use malleable materials with increasing control. (Physical Development)
Group size
Small groups.

Bring in a selection of brightly-coloured costume jewellery to show to the children. Invite them to explore the patterns, colours and designs of the jewellery. Which patterns and colours do they like the best?

Give each child a copy of the photocopiable sheet. Talk about the pictures of the jewellery. Provide them with some modelling materials such as Plasticine or play dough and ask them to choose one of the jewellery pieces to make. Let younger children experiment with the dough or

Plasticine before you ask them to copy one of the simpler pieces. Ask older children to make up some of their own designs. Can they draw it for others to copy?

PAGE 77
CARNIVAL MASKS

Learning objective
To explore colour, texture and shape. (Creative Development)
Group size
Small groups.

Share a book with the children such as *Nini at Carnival* by Lloyd Errol (Red Fox). Have any of the children been to a street carnival? Explain that carnivals are times when people celebrate and wear special clothes and often masks. Give each child a copy of the photocopiable sheet (copied onto card) and explain that they are going to cut out and decorate the mask.

Work with small groups of children and talk about the types of mask that they could create, such as animals or favourite story characters. Encourage them to be really imaginative in their designs – adding collage materials, extra card, paper and so on. Hold a story or animal carnival in the grounds of your setting by playing music, providing drinks and letting the children parade in their masks.

PAGE 78
SOCK CREATURES

Learning objective
To use materials and tools imaginatively. (Creative Development)
Group size
Small groups.

Ask each child to bring in an old sock to make a sock puppet. Make one yourself by sticking on the features from the photocopiable sheet and adding some wool as hair. Give your sock puppet a name and introduce him to the children.

Give each child a copy of the photocopiable sheet and explain that they can colour and cut out some of the features from the sheet to add to their sock puppet. Provide some additional materials such as wool and shredded paper and help the children to stick on some hair. Younger children will need help to cut out the small features but should be encouraged to arrange them on their sock themselves.

Special clothes

◆ Talk about the pictures.

I can...

◆ Colour in the stripes when you can do these things.

I can put on my coat.

I can put on my shoes.

I can do up buttons.

I can do up a zip.

I can put on my apron.

Colour the clothes

◆ Draw arrows between the clothes that begin with the same letter sound. Use a different colour for each pair.

Getting dressed

◆ Cut out the pictures. Put them in order and tell the story.

Designer T-shirts

◆ Finish the patterns on the T-shirts.

Price it up

◆ Use the price tag and price list in the 'clothes shop'.

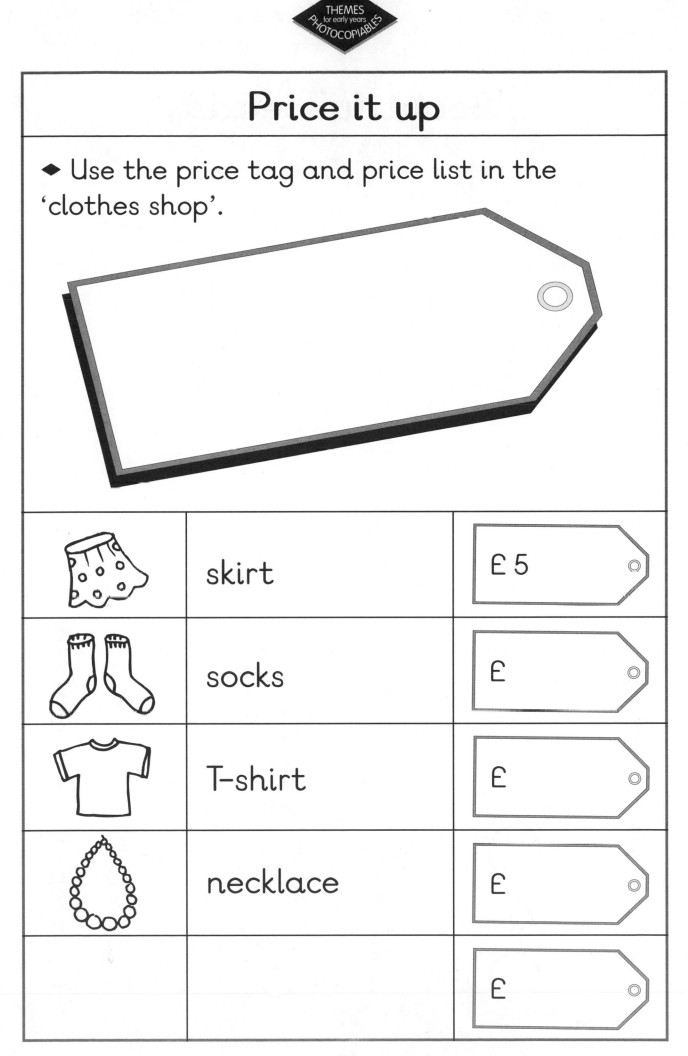

	skirt	£ 5
	socks	£
	T-shirt	£
	necklace	£
		£

Beautiful beads

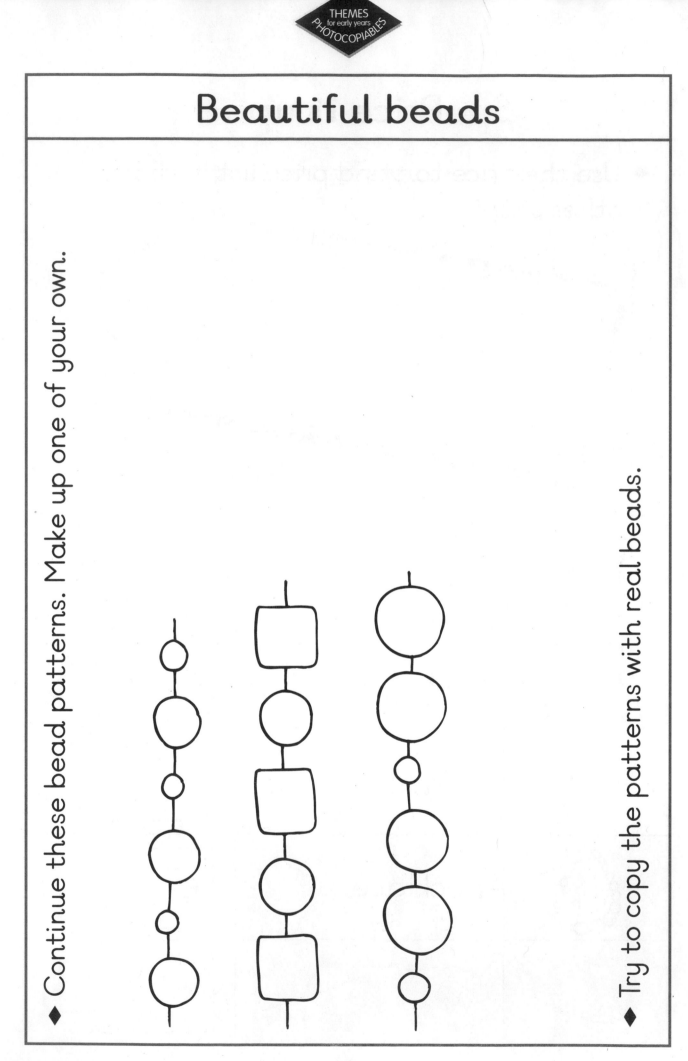

◆ Continue these bead patterns. Make up one of your own.

◆ Try to copy the patterns with real beads.

Spots on bow ties

◆ Count or add spots on the bow ties.

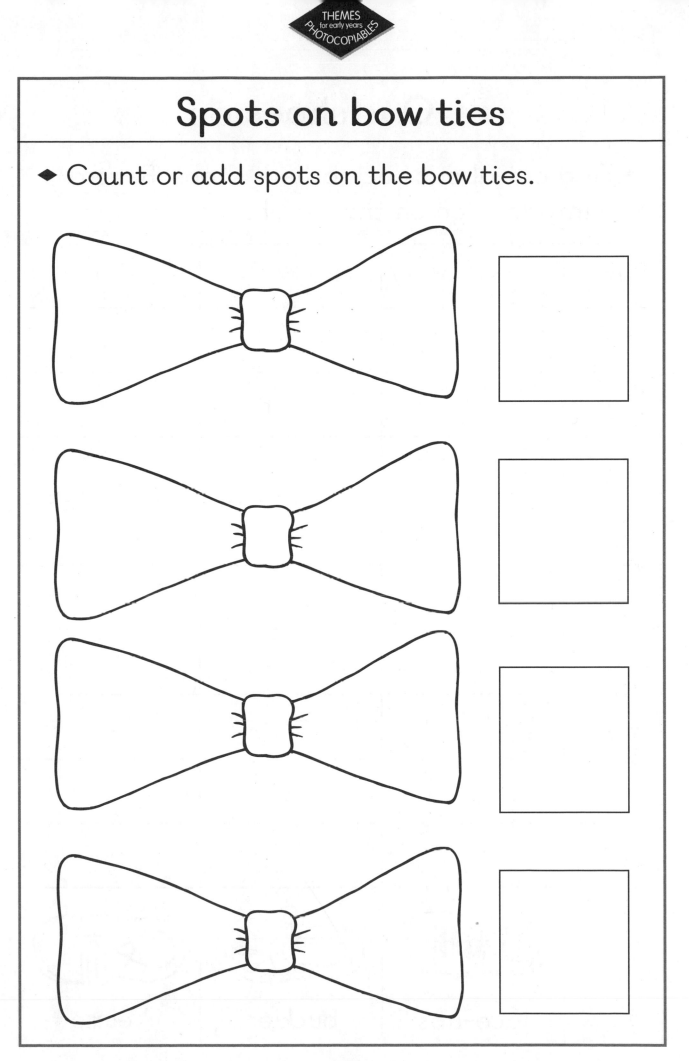

Our shoes

◆ Find out about each other's shoes. Record the information on this graph.

10			
9			
8			
7			
6			
5			
4			
3			
2			
1			
	lace-ups	buckles	Velcro

Rain or shine?

◆ Match the clothes to the sunshine or rain.

Clothes timeline

◆ Cut out the pictures. Put them in order from baby to grown-up.

Lace it up

◆ Sew the pattern onto the trousers.

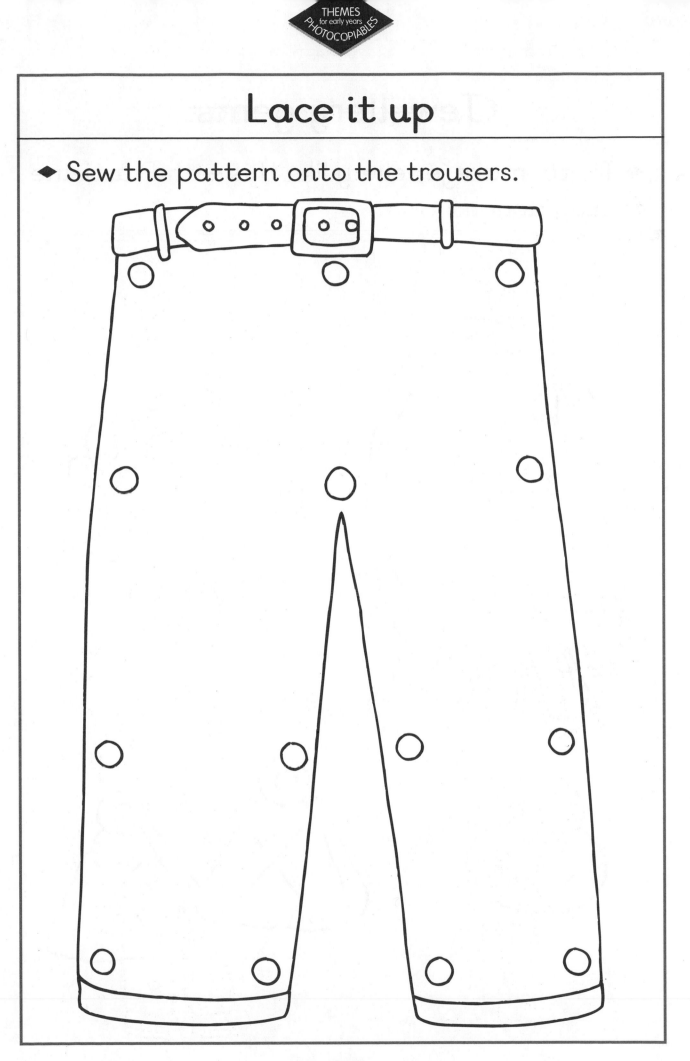

Jewellery gems

◆ Try to make jewellery like this with Plasticine or play dough.

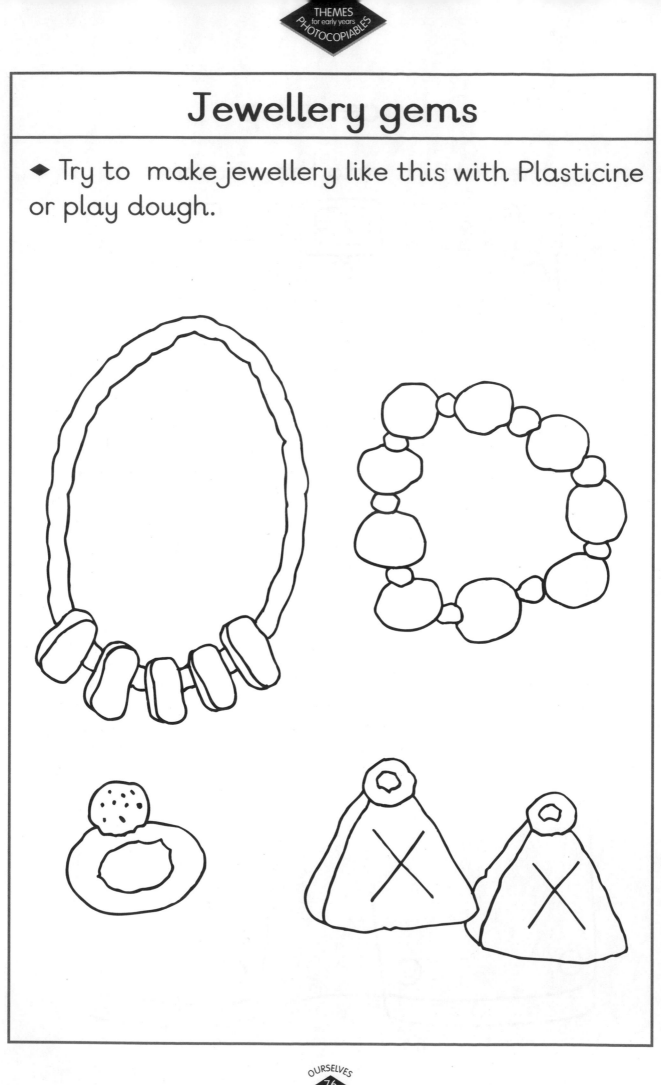

Carnival masks

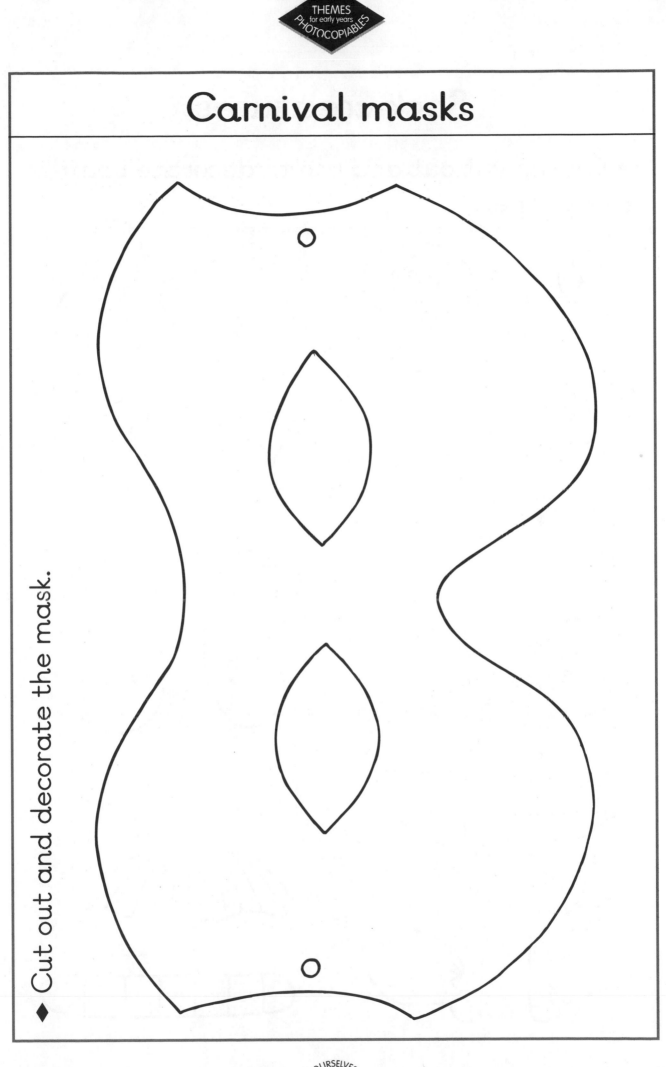

◆ Cut out and decorate the mask.

Sock creatures

◆ Colour, cut out and use to decorate your sock puppet.

FOOD

PAGE 82

MEALTIMES

Learning objective
To develop understanding of appropriate behaviour. (Personal, Social and Emotional Development)
Group size
Whole group.

Read the story of *The Tiger Who Came to Tea* by Judith Kerr (Picture Lions). Ask the children what they thought of the tiger's manners. Was it rude of him to eat all the buns on the plate? What should he have done? Enlarge the photocopiable sheet, which shows a family mealtime, and show it to the children. Are the children in the picture behaving nicely? Why? Use the picture to generate a discussion about a number of social behaviours, such as helping others, hygiene and sharing.

PAGE 83

STORY-TELLING

Learning objective
To respond to and tell stories. (Language and Literacy)
Group size
Whole group/ individuals.

Enlarge a copy of the photocopiable sheet and show the children the pictures at story time. Do the children recognize the stories? (*The Gingerbread Boy*; *Hansel and Gretel*; *Snow White and the Seven Dwarfs* and *The Enormous Turnip*.) Tell a different one to the children each day (they can be found in many good anthologies), encouraging them to remember the story before you begin and to answer questions about the story when you have finished. Let individual children carefully colour the pictures and leave them in the story corner (with finger puppets if possible) to encourage the children to retell the story themselves.

PAGE 84

FROM A-TO-ZUCCHINI

Learning objectives
To develop letter shape and sound recognition. (Language and Literacy)
Group size
Small groups.

Enlarge a copy of the photocopiable sheet and explain to the children that you are going to make a food alphabet together, showing food or drink beginning with every letter of the alphabet. Start by asking each child in turn to say the name of a favourite food. What letter does it begin with? Ask the child to find the letter on the alphabet sheet if appropriate. Scribe the word in the space on the sheet, and ask the child to draw the picture next to it. Now, try to fill in as many letters of the alphabet as possible (using word books and picture dictionaries to help). Let older children work in pairs to attempt the alphabet.

PAGE 85

IN THE BAG

Learning objective
To develop visual memory for pre-reading skills. (Language and Literacy)
Group size
Small groups.

Sit in a small circle with the children and make sure that each child can see the photocopiable sheet clearly. Together, identify all the objects in the bag. Now, explain that you are going to cover up one of the objects, and you would like the children to try to work out which object you have hidden. Let the children look at the bag for a minute or two before covering up one of the pictures. Repeat the game several times.

Play a version of *Kim's Game* with older children, by covering all the objects and asking them to try to remember them all.

PAGE 86
LOOKS TASTY

Learning objective
To use pictures, symbols and familiar words and letters to communicate meaning. (Language and Literacy)
Group size
Up to six children.

Look at a selection of boxes and tins of food with the children. Can they guess what the foods are? How can they tell? Explain that the words and pictures help us to choose what things to buy when we go to the shops. Give each child a copy of the photocopiable sheet. Talk about the shapes of the packages and ask the children to imagine what might go inside. Ask them to draw or write labels (depending on ability) for the packages so that people will know what is in them.

PAGE 87
MATCH THE PAIRS

Learning objective
To develop matching skills and learn about pairs. (Mathematics)
Group size
Small groups.

Give each child a copy of the photocopiable sheet and identify all the pictures together. Demonstrate that each of the pictures is part of a pair, for example by saying, 'The cake goes with the candles'. Let each child cut out their pictures and ask them to choose two pictures that they think are a pair. They may choose any two pictures providing they can explain why they go together. Ask older children to put all the cards into pairs and then let them use the cards with a partner to play games of *Snap* and *Pelmanism*.

PAGE 88
CAKE COUNTING

Learning objective
To develop awareness of number operations. (Mathematics)
Group size
Small groups.

Introduce the activity by singing some counting rhymes such as 'Five currant buns' with the children. Then use the photocopiable sheet in a number of ways to reinforce different mathematical skills, or to target different abilities, such as:
• count the chocolate drops on the cakes
• cut the cakes out and put them in order of number of chocolate drops
• add extra chocolate drops to the cakes to make each one have seven (or a number of your choice)
• throw a dice and cover up a cake that matches the number thrown
• play games of pairs to encourage the children to count carefully.

PAGE 89
ICE-CREAM FLAVOURS

Learning objective
To solve practical problems using mathematical understanding. (Mathematics)
Group size
Small groups.

Introduce the activity by working practically with three different colours of counters. Give each child three coloured counters at a time and ask them to put the counters down in their preferred order. Ask the children to draw and colour what they see. Ask the next child to use the same three colours and put them down in a different order. Again, ask the children to record what they see. Encourage the group to find all the combinations. Now give each child a copy of the photocopiable sheet and let them choose three colours (flavours) to make each ice-cream cup different.

PAGE 90
FOOD SHAPES

Learning objective
To explore knowledge of shapes and to develop mathematical language. (Mathematics)
Group size
Small groups.

Put some fruit and vegetables into a feely bag and ask the children to take it in turns to come and feel a piece of food, describe it and try to guess what it is. When all the children have had a turn, provide each child with a copy of the photocopiable sheet. Ask individual children to choose a parcel to describe and guess what is inside. Let the children draw the objects onto the parcels when they have guessed.

PAGE 91
PIZZA PARTY

Learning objective
To develop comparing and counting skills. (Mathematics)
Group size
Four children.

Explain that you are going to have a pizza party, and you would like the children's help to make sure that everyone gets the same amount of topping on their pizza and the same number of slices. Give each child a copy of the photocopiable sheet and together count the number of mushrooms, peas and so on. Ask the children to draw the same number of things on each of the other three slices. When they have finished, let them cut out their pizza slices and ask them to give a slice to every child. Each child will have four pieces to put together to make a whole pizza! Ask older children to count how many peas/mushrooms and so on they have altogether.

PAGE 92
KEEP THE RECIPE

Learning objective
To explore and record change in a cookery activity. (Knowledge and Understanding of the World)
Group size
Small groups.

This photocopiable sheet provides a template for the children to use to record cookery activities. Ask them to draw or write down the equipment and ingredients that they used. In the space at the bottom of the sheet, invite younger children to draw a picture of the finished product and older children to draw two pictures to show the raw mixture and the final version.

PAGE 93
SWEET WRAPPERS

Learning objective
To use malleable materials with increasing control. (Physical Development)
Group size
Small groups.

Provide a selection of different-coloured pieces of Plasticine or play dough. Working with groups of children, demonstrate how to manipulate the dough and invite the children to copy some of the shapes you make. Give each child a copy of the photocopiable sheet and ask them to make some sweets and lollipops to fit on top of the wrappers. Ask older children to colour the wrappers to match their sweets.

PAGE 94
PLAN A PICNIC

Learning objective
To use imagination to plan a picnic. (Creative Development)
Group size
Small groups.

Sit in a circle with a group of children and play a memory game together. Ask them to think of things to take on a picnic. Each child has to remember the previous list of things and add a new thing to the list. For example: 'We are going on a picnic and we will take a sandwich, a rug and a ball...' and so on. Now, give each child a copy of the photocopiable sheet and help them to make up their own list of things to take on a picnic, putting toys, food and other things in the appropriate spaces. Let younger children draw one thing in each category and ask older children to try to write some words as well as drawing pictures.

PAGE 95
WIGGLY CATERPILLAR

Learning objective
To use a range of materials and instruments to make a model for use in imaginative play. (Creative Development)
Group size
Up to four children.

Read the story *The Very Hungry Caterpillar* by Eric Carle (Picture Puffin) to the children. Talk about all the things that he ate. What are the children's favourite foods? Explain that the children are going to make their own wiggly caterpillar. Copy the photocopiable sheet onto thin, coloured card and provide each child with a copy. Help the children to cut out the discs, thread a tapestry needle with thick cotton, then pierce and thread the discs together, separating each disc with a pasta tube to make the caterpillar wiggle.

Provide a selection of pretend food and a copy of the story in the story corner and encourage the children to act out the story using their wiggly caterpillars.

PAGE 96
PLAYING THE SPOONS

Learning objective
To use everyday objects to explore sound and simple musical composition. (Creative Development)
Group size
Small groups.

Provide a selection of everyday (safe) cooking utensils to match the pictures on the photocopiable sheet (spatula, plastic pot, balloon whisk and wooden spoon). Let the children investigate the sounds that they can make with them. After they have explored the 'instruments' ask individual children to cut out the pictures on their sheet and put them in a line. Can they play the 'instruments' in this order? Ask the children to take it in turns to put their pictures down in an order for the others to follow.

Provide extra copies of the sheet for older children and encourage them to invent more complicated and extended musical patterns.

Mealtimes

◆ Talk about the picture.

Story-telling

◆ Tell the stories in the pictures.

From a-to-zucchini

◆ Think of some food or drink for each letter.

a		n	
b		o	
c		p	
d		q	quorn
e		r	
f		s	
g		t	
h		u	
i		v	
j		w	
k		x	xmas pud
l		y	
m		z	zucchini

In the bag

◆ Look carefully at the picture. Cover it up.
What food can you remember?

Looks tasty

◆ Draw or write labels for the food containers.

Match the pairs

◆ Cut out the cards and make pairs.

Cake counting

◆ Count the chocolate drops on the cakes.

Ice-cream flavours

◆ Use three colours to try to make each
ice-cream different.

Food shapes

◆ Describe the parcels. Guess what food is inside.

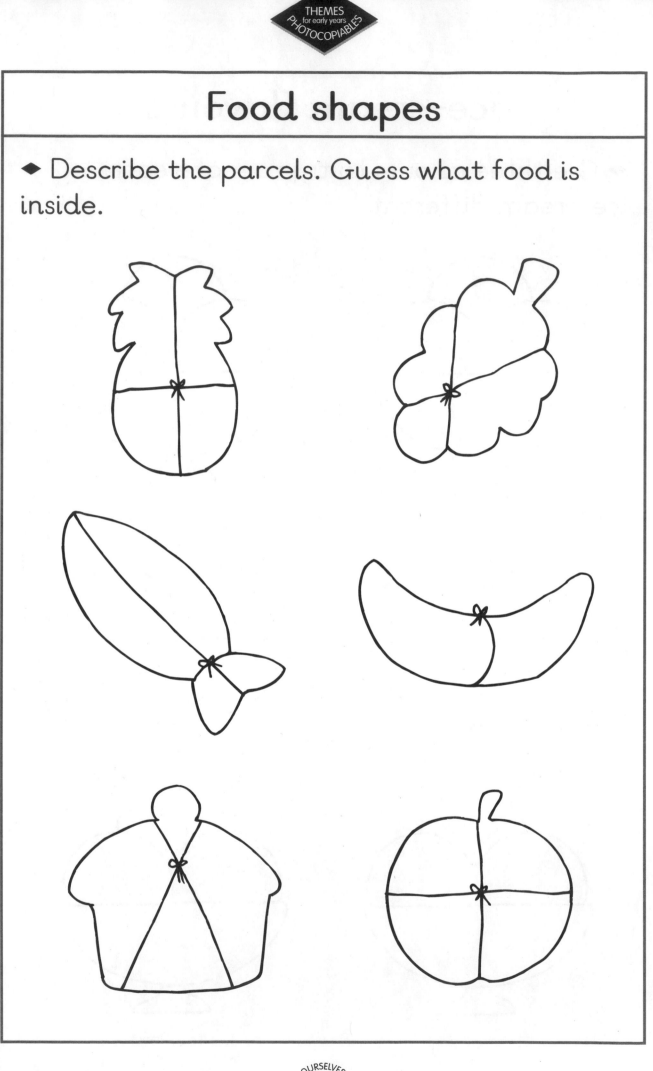

Pizza party

◆ Give each slice of pizza the same topping.

Keep the recipe

A recipe for _____

equipment	ingredients

how it looks

Sweet wrappers

◆ Use Plasticine to make some sweets to fit
the wrappers. Colour the wrappers to match.

Plan a picnic

◆ Draw or write in the boxes to plan a picnic.

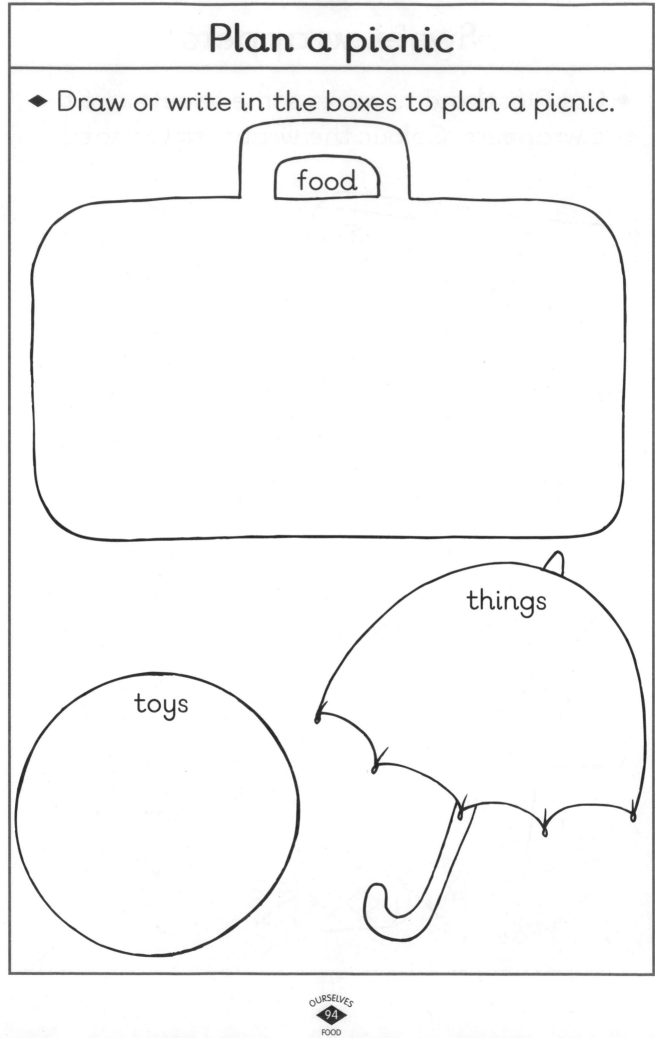

food

things

toys

Wiggly caterpillar

◆ Cut out the shapes and thread together with pasta to make a wiggly caterpillar.

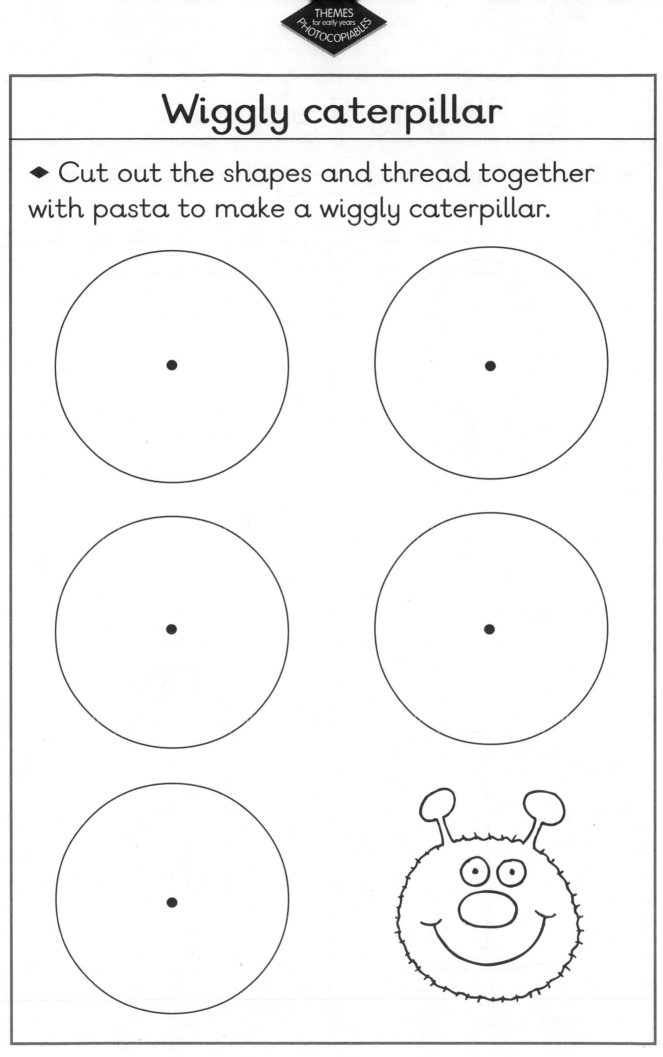

Playing the spoons

◆ Cut out the pictures. Put them in playing order.